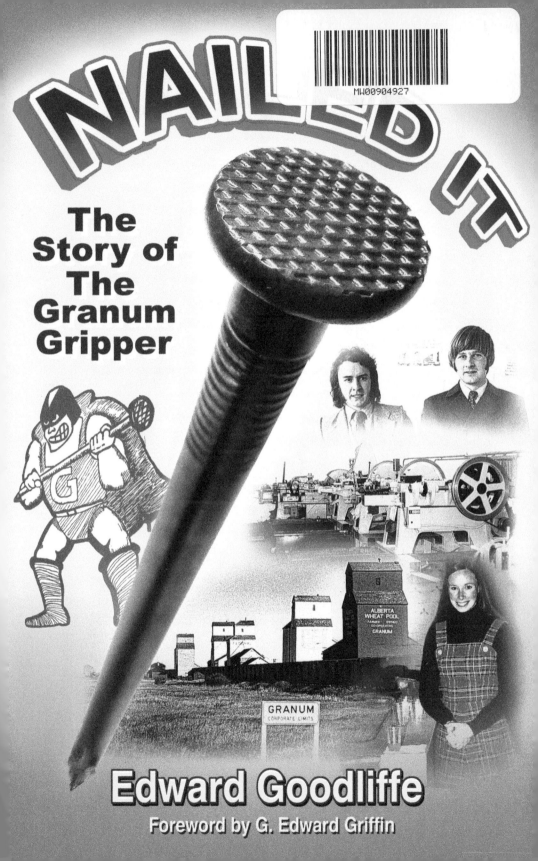

NAILED IT

The Story of The Granum Gripper

GRANUM
CORPORATE LIMITS

Edward Goodliffe

Foreword by G. Edward Griffin

Outskirts Press, Inc.
http://www.outskirtspress.com

Paperback ISBN: 978-1-9772-1593-2
Hardback ISBN: 978-1-9772-1594-9

TABLE OF CONTENTS

ACKNOWLEDGMENTS

I WOULD LIKE to thank three people for their assistance in making this book a reality. Ken Gullekson for his guidance on storytelling and book publishing. G. Edward Griffin for taking the time and trouble to read my story as it progressed and for all the useful tips and encouragement. And finally, David Dees who took a very crude sketch of what I thought would make a good cover and turned it into an artistic masterpiece.

FOREWORD

WHEN EDWARD GOODLIFFE sent me the journal of his early days in the nail-manufacturing business and asked if I thought anyone would want to read it if it were a small book, my initial reaction was to find a way to gently break the news to him that a book about making nails didn't quite sound like a blockbuster.

Before responding, I thought I should at least scan the manuscript so I could honestly say I was familiar with the story but, to my great surprise, Edward's congenial style and total recall of details immediately captured my full attention. This was not about machines making nails but about the human spirit overcoming obstacles. Before I knew it, I was on page 14 and anxious to discover what would happen next.

You will enjoy this story because, although it is not heroic in the sense of classical literature, it is about the everyday heroism of one couple with good will toward all and endowed by the capacity for hard work and childlike curiosity who splash through life making the world a better place than they found it – and having a lot of fun along the way.

The phrase "roll models" comes to mind.

G. Edward Griffin. July 2nd 2019
gegriffin31@gmail.com

Introduction

Universal Nail factory in 1984

IT HAS NOW been thirty-four years since the machines fell silent. Such a long time in fact that it feels a little like it happened in a previous life. So much time has elapsed that most of the residents of the Granum area during that period are now dead, and so the story of Universal Nail and the Granum Gripper has largely slipped from living memory. I realize that if the tale is to be preserved at all, and I think it should be, the responsibility lands squarely on my shoulders to make it happen, as I, with the exception of my wife, Jane, am the only one who knows the whole story.

In those days, I was a young man. Now I am not, and should I die tomorrow, the whole amazing adventure would go unrecorded, and nobody would really know what happened in that strangely shaped building just east of where the train track used to run.

Today Taco Hansma runs his High Plains Hoof Care business from the front half of the old nail factory and Owen Alcock has his mechanical workshop in the back. Owen came from Zimbabwe (formally Southern Rhodesia) after his farm was stolen from him by the communist Mugabe regime. The story of what Owen lived through is absolutely heartbreaking and could fill a book. It would have destroyed most people, but Owen is no ordinary man. To any passing stranger, the old factory looks much like any other industrial building: one hundred feet long, forty feet wide, and twelve feet high in the front half, and eighteen feet at the peak in the back.

For those who know the history, the telltale evidence is still there to see. The location of the first Wafios S110 nail machine that was bolted to the floor, almost in the middle of the original forty-by-fifty-foot building, can be easily located. That was the spot where the mayor Ege Mohr together with many Granum residents gathered to watch the machine in action at the official start of production. Over against the east wall at the south end of the original building, you can see where the Wafios S110 was subsequently moved and next to it the location of the Glader Number 2 nail machine. It was in that corner where Mayor Mohr gave his speech at the party to celebrate surviving the first two years of business. The concrete is substantially worn where oil drums filled with nails had been dragged out from beneath the production chutes. Grease marks are clearly visible up the east wall, where the grease had been thrown from the main cranks that ran at about 325 strokes a minute. Another interesting relic is the sight of nails stuck in the ceiling. That happened when the spring on the Glader's ejector blade broke one day while the machine was running.

The function of the ejector blade is to deflect the nail that has just been formed down the chute and out of the way before the header cold forges the head on the next nail. With no ejector to move the nail, the header smacked into the newly made nails at great speed and propelled them all over the place, some of them ending up stuck in the ceiling.

In the newer part of the building, it is easy to spot the hole in the ceiling where the exhaust from the McCormick Deering Diesel was vented. That was the power source for the bull block that drew the wire the nails were made from. The west wall of the newer building still has the electrical conduit indicating where the four nail machines and the Humphrey fence staple machine were located. The office is still there on that west side just into the newer part of the building. On the west side in the original part of the building, there are marks on the floor that show where the nail tumbler was, as well as the acid coating tank and the spin dryer. Above, you can see the chimney vent from the acid tank.

(1)

The Beginning

Where exactly do I start? It seems that life is a journey along a road with many Y junctions. There are so many choices along the way, but somehow we are programmed to strive for certain things, and our choices can lead us inexorably to that end.

I was born in London, England, in 1949. I was the youngest of six children and grew up just outside suburbia near Lingfield in Surrey, which was about halfway between London and Eastbourne on the south coast.

At the age of eight, I was sent to boarding school; The Hawthorns at Gatton Point, Redhill run by the Bull family. Sounds so very British; mind you it was not John Bull that ran the school, but Dudley, and Christopher Bull, and their

sister Margaret was the matron. She had a very agreeable wired hair terrier dog called Paddy. I can remember good old Paddy doing me a great favour one lunchtime when 'stodge' (suet pudding) was served for dessert. The thought of having to eat that was more than I could handle, and I was considering hiding it in my pocket, but I was saved by Paddy who was wandering by and he sorted out my problem. Looking back on those days, I realize that they did a very good job of teaching us important things like good manners, how to speak properly, write properly and good sportsmanship. Like the other two schools I attended, we were taught to unquestionably do what we were told. I have since realized that it is essential to question everything, think for yourself and be prepared to ignore immoral, evil or just plain stupid directives. Too many people carry out wicked deeds, and their excuse is that they were just following orders. We are responsible for our own actions, and so we must have the courage to defy bad directives and laws.

At school, I was not considered a bright student, but when it came to geography, I was good at that. Those countries that were coloured red were the British Commonwealth, places where I could expect people to speak the same language and possibly have the same sort of values that I had been brought up to have. Now they were fascinating. Canada seemed to hold such promise, that vast expanse of land with very few people. Britain was so crowded, and the taxes were so high; in fact the top rate of income tax in the early 1970s was 95 percent, and land prices were prohibitive. I really wanted to live in a rural area and have lots of land to enjoy, and there was little chance of me being able to have that in Britain. Those places on the map were so intriguing; what could they possibly be like?

In 1960, my sister Ann headed off to Canada to explore. She had a wonderful time and never came back to live in England. She now resides in Calgary. In 1965, my father and mother took me to Canada with my sisters Marg and Sue. It was an incredible trip: we sailed from Southampton on the Cunard ship HMS *Carmania,* which sailed to Le Havre, in France; Cobh, in Ireland; Quebec City; and then Montreal.

During the five-day crossing, there was a table tennis tournament, and a lot of passengers signed up for it. Both my father and I continued to win our matches and met in the semifinal. A huge crowd turned out to watch us play the best of five games, and I just managed to beat him. The final was easy; I was up against someone who loved smashing the ball at great speed but was totally unprepared to have it returned to a part of the table she could not reach, and I beat her easily. I still have the pewter tankard with the *Carmania* crest on it that I won that day.

After disembarking in Montreal and spending a few days with Ann and her husband, Jim, we went to Ottawa, Toronto, and Niagara Falls before flying west to Vancouver on an Air Canada Vickers Vanguard.

After a ferry ride to Victoria, we had tea at the Empress Hotel where we met Great-Uncle Arthur, my mother's uncle. That was an interesting meeting, as Great-Uncle Arthur had migrated to Canada in the very early years of the twentieth century, first homesteading in Manitoba. Later he sold his quarter and purchased a bigger piece of land in Saskatchewan, where he farmed for many years before retiring in Victoria.

Vancouver was a beautiful city. There were not many high-rise buildings at that time. The Bayshore Inn had just been built, and the tallest buildings that I remember were the Vancouver Hotel and the Marine Building down by the waterfront. The train journey through to Banff was spectacular. The Banff area was beautiful. Calgary was interesting; they named the main roads trails: the Glenmore Trail, Crowchild Trail, Macleod Trail, and Deerfoot Trail, etc. It sounded like it was a new frontier. Regina, Saskatchewan, was quite an experience, and a visit to a nearby farm was amazing. I had never seen such a vast expanse of fine-looking wheat. Talk about flat terrain; it was flatter than a pancake. There were no food shortages in that place.

From Regina we got back onto the Vickers Vanguard and flew to Montreal, where we boarded the HMS *Franconia* for the voyage back to Southampton. The seed was sown, not so much for Ontario or Quebec but for the western provinces—now there was the promised land.

Fast-forward a few years and I had left school and qualified in automotive engineering in London in preparation for going into the family contract cleaning business, specifically in the area of managing the fleet of cars, trucks, and vans. My father was partially retired at that time, and Uncle George was in charge. I did not quite see eye to eye with Uncle George. I was putting in long hours doing mundane jobs that seemed to have no purpose. It appeared that I was just getting sidelined while other members of the family were being groomed for important positions. Things were not looking good, so I started to work on plan B.

I teamed up with a friend I had made during the time I was at engineering college by the name of Lachlan Grant Young. Grant, an extraordinary, larger-than-life character, was studying aeronautical engineering and, after becoming qualified in the field, concluded that there was no future in that endeavour.

My friendship with Grant had developed because of our similar views on the free market and individual liberty. Frequently during lectures, I would disagree with the collectivist viewpoint put forward, and I would speak up. Grant would soon join in to support me. The same thing would happen when he spoke up to voice his opinion; invariably, I would agree with him and would support his position.

Grant had gone off and joined the sales team at the Abbey Life Assurance Company and was doing well selling life assurance. After discussions with him about my tenuous position in the family business and his dissatisfaction with being an employee of Abbey Life, we decided to join forces and form a limited company of our own.

Over the following weeks, the two of us undertook several fundraising activities to bankroll the cost of incorporating the company. On hot days we picked up cases of canned soft drinks at King's Cross Cash and Carry and headed to a beach on the south coast called Camber Sands where we sold the cold drinks at a substantial markup. After all costs, we made a fairly good return but could not do that for long because of harassment from the authorities, who expected us to pay a fee for licenses, which we never did.

One highly profitable venture was on the day of the Lingfield point-to-point horse races. The entrance to the event was just a few hundred yards down the road from where we lived, and our property included an orchard filled with apple and plum trees, which we decided would be great for parking cars. The racecourse was charging one pound per vehicle to park, which was a lot of money in those days, so we quickly painted a sign that said "Parking 50 Pence" per vehicle and put it up outside our gate as soon as my father drove off to play golf that Saturday morning. Grant and I put on our white coats so we looked official, and in no time we had vehicles turning in to take advantage of the cheap parking. It did not take long before the racecourse people were over complaining, but we soon told them where to get off and continued until the place was full.

When my father arrived back from golf, he was absolutely horrified by what he saw and promptly grilled me on exactly what I thought I was up to. His anger soon subsided. He asked how much we had made and was very impressed at our business acumen. He said that it could be a bit awkward when he next saw the owners of the racecourse down at the pub, but he decided to let them know that he had thoroughly berated me for this unwarranted behaviour, and he had made me give the proceeds to charity. At that point, I was devastated; we had done all that for nothing? "Oh no," he said, "that is what I am going to tell them. I won't mention that charity begins at home."

It wasn't long before we had our limited company set up. I was chairman and Grant was managing director. Not long after that, Uncle George decided that he wanted me out of the way, and I was to be sent off to Germany for two years. I did not want to do that. In the interest of brevity, suffice it to say, I upset him mightily and he fired me. My father was furious and told me to get out. That I did without delay and went straight to London, where I stayed for a few days with my good friend Michael Hobden as I got organized. Michael was living above a stable near Hyde Park; the address was 32 Grosvenor Crescent Mews. The stink of the horses was rank, and one of the most memorable things about the place was that it had an original Thomas Crapper, who was famous for his flushing toilet in the 1800s. It was a substantial piece of equipment that had a huge cast-iron tank near the ceiling, with his name emblazoned in the casting, and a 1½-inch lead pipe running down to the toilet bowl. On vigorously pulling the chain, a thunderous roar of water would ensue washing everything away and waking anyone who might be asleep in the building.

I soon found myself somewhere to live and a vehicle to drive, thanks to the friendship I had made with secondhand-car dealer Jim Gallard. who supplied me with an Austin Mini traveller at a very reasonable price.

We secured an agreement with newly formed Hambro Life Assurance Company to be an independent broker for the company and went out selling life assurance. I knew absolutely nothing about life assurance, but a few hours of training from Grant and an in-depth study of the rate book and I was ready to go.

The next three years were the wildest ride you could ever imagine. I learned more in those three years than at any other time of my life. It was excruciating at times,

Grant and Edward at Anerley Road

and when you consider that I don't like big cities, it was not a great place for me to be. We started with a rented office at 69 Anerley Road, Crystal Palace, London, SE 19.

Later we moved to 4 Camberwell Green, London, SE 5, in one of the less salubrious parts of London, just south of the Elephant & Castle down

Walworth Road. Number four was on a terrace along the west side of the green. There were shops on the ground floor, and there was a first and second floor. Number four had a third floor above it, so when you looked at the building from the green, it appeared to have a lump on the top. Jane named 4 Camberwell Green "the wart." We all thought the name suited the place well, so from that moment on, it was referred to as the wart. I do recall many occasions when I

The Wart

mentioned that I was going back to the wart in front of strangers, and you could see by their faces that they were wondering. "What on earth is the wart?"

I lived in "the boardroom" upstairs from the office, the actual wart. It was a very decrepit building, owned by Melhuish Flour, which had an adjoining warehouse. The rent was incredibly low because it was in such poor shape. I think it was put up sometime in the mid 1800s. The floors sagged so badly that they were about a foot lower in the middle of the room than at the edges. In one of the rooms, there was a huge hole in the wall where the plaster had fallen to the floor exposing the wooden slats, and we counted about ten layers of wallpaper that had been applied since the building was erected. We rented the top two floors, and although on the top floor there was a bathroom and a kitchen, which actually were the same room, you had to go all the way to the ground floor and out into the backyard to get to the toilet. In the room we used for the office, vagrants had been urinating and defecating on the floor, and it took quite a lot of scrubbing to clean it up. After thoroughly washing it, we sanded the floor boards and varnished them, which sorted out the problem.

In the retail shop on the ground floor, Bob Jarman sold posters. Behind it was a storeroom that you had to go through to reach the backyard where the toilet was. There was a mildly insane woman by the name of Margaret Mitchell who lived on the first floor. She continually warned us about the danger of the ghosts and the "pipe dragons" that lived in the building, and she thought that the Second World War was still on. She assured us that she was a personal friend of Adolph Hitler, so we would be all right. Mad as she was, she was right about the building being haunted.

This has nothing to do with nails and is a total sidetrack, but I suspect you will forgive me for digressing even more than I have already because this is a fascinating little story:

I had recently met Jane, who later migrated to Canada with me and became my wife. We raised three children together, and she helped me make Universal Nail go.

It was a Friday, and I had invited her over for the evening. At that time Bob Jarman was doing some renovations to his shop and had about a hundred two-by-four studs in the way stacked part way into his storeroom and obstructing the door. It was a long corridor that connected the staircase and the door to the street. Under the staircase, there was a door to the cellar. If you opened that door, there was a drop of about eight feet as the old staircase had long since rotted away. It always felt cold near that door. At one point during the evening, I told Jane that I was going downstairs to the toilet, and off I went through the door by the cellar, through Bob's storeroom, and finally through the door to the yard. While I was in the toilet, I heard the door close. That seemed strange as there was no wind, and I did not think that there was anyone else around. When I came out of the toilet, the door was indeed closed. I opened it expecting to see the light from the passageway beyond Bob's storeroom, but instead there was total darkness. I felt my way through to the second door, and to my amazement, it was closed. How could it possibly be closed when all that lumber was blocking it? I opened it and could see clearly from the passageway light that all the lumber had been moved and stacked neatly along the wall.

I rushed upstairs and asked Jane where the lumber had been stacked, and of course she told me that it was part way through the door. She went straight down to witness what had happened. "Something" moved about one hundred studs and stacked them neatly and did it in about two minutes. Impossible, you would think, and yet it happened. On Monday morning, Bob came into the office and thanked me for rearranging his lumber so neatly, and I told him what had happened. He did not believe me. Are there ghostly spirits that can move things? After that experience, I would not hesitate to say yes.

Before getting back to the original story, I will just mention one more thing about London before moving on to Western Canada, and that is regarding my application to migrate to Canada. In light of recent events regarding mass migration from Third World countries replacing white populations, it is interesting to note what was revealed to me all those years ago.

When I went for my interview at the Canadian High Commission in Grosvenor Square, the man I saw was a very French Quebecker. In order to have a good chance of having my application to migrate approved, it was necessary to have documentation demonstrating that I had a job to go to. I did not, as I planned to create my own employment. He was not inclined to believe me, so I pointed out that I had my own business in London, and it was my intention to create my own job in Canada. That was still not good enough for him, and he requested documented proof to demonstrate that I did indeed have a business and sufficient assets to do what I said I was going to do. After returning with paperwork proving that I had the capability of doing that, he told me there were quotas that could not be exceeded. He advised me that for the current year (1974), the quota for white, English-speaking people was filled. The agent laughed as he told me that they still had plenty of quota left for black people, especially if they spoke French.

Looking back on that comment all those years ago, it becomes very clear that there has been a deliberate government policy for a very long time to restrict white, English-speaking people from migrating to Canada from Britain and presumably from everywhere else. To point that out would result in being called a racist, but it is noteworthy that the government of Canada had in place a very racist policy at that time, which appears to have continued for many years, and the result has been most profound. Fortunately, early in the following year, they approved my application.

I now had the green light to migrate to Canada, but there was a daunting problem: the Exchange Control Act of 1947 prohibited anyone from taking cash out of Britain without Bank of England permission. The maximum that anyone could leave the country with was ten pounds in cash and three hundred pounds in traveller's cheques. So by law I was not allowed to take my own money to Alberta. Getting Bank of England permission was out of the question, as I was embroiled in a dispute with the Inland Revenue (UK tax authorities) at the time, so there was a greater chance of me being struck by lightning than getting approval from them.

The penalty for being caught leaving with excess cash was punitive, but on discussing the matter with Grant, he offered to help me if I was willing to chance it. Good old Grant with his nerves of steel. We decided to take thirty thousand pounds in cash, so I kept drawing out large amounts in the biggest denomination banknotes I could get, and then I put them in a large safety deposit box at the Midland Bank in the city not far from the Bank of England. At that time the twenty-pound note was the highest denomination, and it was not always available, so I had to stockpile some ten-pound notes as well. I went into the London branch of the Canadian Imperial Bank of Commerce and asked for an introduction to someone at the main Calgary branch. I was given the name Cec Johnson at the Eighth Avenue branch in the city centre.

We booked tickets to Calgary for January 1975, and I also booked a return ticket to Paris a few days before that. I went to Paris just in case someone had noticed the huge amounts of cash that I had been drawing out and had flagged my name to check me if I attempted to leave the country. Needless to say, the trip to Paris went without incident. The big day was nearly upon us, and we were somewhat apprehensive at the prospect of what we were about to

Jane in the Triumph TR4

do. We went to the Midland Bank and picked up the cash and returned to the wart, where we then tried to conceal this massive pile of banknotes; it was so huge, it was ridiculous. Fortunately, at that time, flared trousers were fashionable, so we strapped the majority of the cash to our legs from the knees down to our ankles, and it did not show at all. The rest was strapped around our waists and in our clothing. Having worked that out, we were ready for action. The next morning we strapped it all on and loaded our luggage into my Triumph TR4 and headed to Heathrow airport.

It was the start of a day to remember, and within minutes we had our first problem. We were driving through Loughborough Junction, which, as anyone who knows London will attest, is not somewhere that you want to be wandering around with large amounts of cash on you at any time of day or night. Well, all of a sudden the accelerator pedal had no effect, and the car came to a stop, but the engine was still ticking over. Grant lifted up the bonnet (hood) and soon discovered that the linkage to the twin Stromberg carburetors had broken off. A few minutes and a bit of tie wire later, and we were back in action driving to the airport with the radio on.

Soon after that we heard an announcement that advised all passengers heading to Heathrow to allow extra time, as there had been a terrorist threat to blow up an El Al (Israeli National Airline) passenger jet, and there was heightened security. In those days security was nothing like it is today, and because of the threat, Her Majesty's Armed Forces had been deployed to handle the situation. As we arrived at Heathrow, there were numerous armoured cars and army personnel with automatic weapons all over the place. We checked our baggage for the Calgary flight, picked up our boarding passes, and were instructed to go to a certain area where we were to be checked over by the military. On our way we passed huge signs warning us that we could not take more than ten pounds in cash and three hundred pounds in traveller's cheques beyond that point. It was a bit nerve-racking to say the least. I was asked a lot of questions and then made to stand with my arms outstretched and my legs apart while he frisked me. My heart was beating so hard, it was exceedingly difficult pretending to be calm. When he was patting me down, he paid particular attention to my lower legs where most of the cash was strapped. He then told me to stand and wait for further instructions in a corner of the room. Grant was already standing there. We were amongst the first to be frisked, so there were just a few of us standing there. In the opposite corner of the room, there was another group that appeared to have more people in it than ours. As the minutes went by, our group became more voluminous and then an announcement was made that those passengers in the largest group, which was our group, could go through to the duty-free shops and our departure gate. The people in the other group would be required to go for a strip search.

We could not believe our good fortune. Grant confirmed that when he was frisked, special attention was made when checking his lower legs too. Why did they let us through? The best explanation we could come up with was because the flight was to Calgary, Alberta. There were quite a lot of passengers with cowboy hats and boots. We were wearing leather shoes, and maybe they thought that we had cowboy boots on, and it was obvious that we did not have firearms attached to our legs. They were probably not looking for concealed money.

We boarded our flight, and it took off. I still felt extremely stressed, and that feeling got a whole lot worse a few minutes into the flight when the captain made an announcement welcoming us on board and apologising for the late departure due to the unexpected security problems. He went on to say that he had been directed to make an unscheduled landing at Prestwick in Scotland and assured us that we would only be stopping for a few minutes.

Well, as you can imagine, that sent us into panic mode, and as it was really hot in the plane, I was sweating so profusely that I think I could have wrung out my shirt.

As the plane approached the runway at Prestwick, several police cars were clearly visible with their lights flashing. The plane did not go to the terminal and just pulled onto the apron. A mobile staircase pulled up to the plane, the door was opened, and two police officers climbed on board. They came down the aisle toward us and arrested two men sitting in front of me. They must have thought that I looked a little hot; I was absolutely drenched and close to having heart failure as was Grant, who was sitting in the row of seats behind me.

Right away they left, and the door was closed. We taxied to the beginning of the runway, and we were off again. By the time we reached the west coast of Greenland, I asked the stewardess to ask the captain if in the event of a problem we would go forward to Gander, Newfoundland, or back to Prestwick, and she came back with confirmation that we would not be going back to Britain. Now that was music to my ears.

You might think that at last our problems had ended, but you would be wrong. We landed in Calgary, and the cabin crew welcomed us there and announced that the local temperature was -10 Fahrenheit. We realized that we did not even have coats with us, let alone gloves or ear muffs; we would not have to worry about sweating anymore.

We cleared customs with no problem and went to get a taxi. It was around midnight, and the Calgary airport was all but dead. We had to wait several minutes for a taxi to turn up and then asked the driver to take us to a hotel. He asked which one, and we did not know, so we said that he could choose one for us. We were really tired, as it had been a very long day, and we did not notice when he dropped us off at the National Hotel that it was a bit run down. As we were checking in, Grant said that he really needed a beer, and he was going to nip off to the bar, pick up a bottle or two, and meet me at the room. I headed up, and a few minutes later a breathless Grant turned up with his beer. He was quite distressed and told me that he had made a terrible mistake. The bar had some very rough-looking people in it, and when he went to pay for the beer, he only had pounds and that caused some confusion and drew attention to him. He told the bartender to keep the change and rushed up to the room. We discussed the situation and wondered whether we should leave or stay. Our minds were soon made up when there was a bang on the door from "room service." We did not open the door and said that we had not asked for any room service. The man on the outside was most insistent that he had something to give me, but I told him I did not want it and to go away, which he did after a few minutes.

We decided that we should leave in case a bunch of them came back and kicked the door in. To go down to the lobby would necessitate us passing the bar, which would not have been a good idea, so we decided that the fire escape would be a better option. We got prepared to leave, and Grant got hold of a chair to use as a weapon as I opened the door. There was nobody there so he put the chair down, and we headed down the hallway out of the fire escape door, and down the metal staircase to the ground. By that time it was about one in the morning. The cold was absolutely numbing, and there was virtually no traffic. About two blocks ahead there seemed to be quite a few vehicles going by, so we walked briskly down the road in that direction. Fortunately it was not long before a taxi on that busy road was crossing the one we were on and did a sharp turn and came toward us. The driver pulled down his window and asked what on earth we were doing walking down the road at one in the morning with suitcases and no coats when it was so cold? Without delay, we climbed in his car and asked him to take us to the best hotel in town. He told us that the Four Seasons had just opened, and that is where he took us. We explained to him what had happened, and he was horrified. He explained that he had been aware of some unscrupulous taxi drivers who had been taking unsuspecting tourists to the National Hotel where they had been beaten up and robbed. It seems we had been fortunate to avoid that fate.

The following day we went to see Cec Johnson at the bank. He was a most jovial fellow, and I filled in the paperwork to open an account. When that was done, he advised me that it would be necessary to make a deposit to activate the account; just a few dollars would be sufficient. I told him that actually I had rather a lot to deposit and proceeded to pile up a mountain of banknotes. Cec was highly entertained with the whole thing and said he had never experienced anything quite like what happened that day. It took a long time to count it all out, and after that, he took us to lunch.

I stayed in touch with Cec for a few years and then lost contact with him. About a decade ago, I decided to give him a call because I still had his home telephone number. It was rather a distressing call. He answered and sounded just the same as I remembered. I told him who I was, and it meant nothing to him. He apologised and told me that he had Alzheimer's. What a shame, poor old Cec.

After doing the banking, I telephoned my sister Ann who was absolutely shocked to hear that we were in Calgary and promptly invited us to stay, which we did. Dear Ann, despite zero notice of our arrival, made us most welcome.

(2)

ARRIVAL IN ALBERTA

THERE WE WERE in May 1975, Grant, Jane, and I crammed into our 1974 Datsun pickup truck that we had just purchased from Bow Ridge Motors in Cochrane, touring the small towns of southern Alberta looking for the perfect place to set up our proposed nail factory.

We had arrived at the end of April from London and spent our first few weeks with my sister Ann, her husband, Jim, and their children, Mark, Nadine, and Stephen. Our few possessions had been packed into three tea chests and were on their way by sea and not expected to arrive for a month or so.

Our original plan was to set up some sort of business, preferably manufacturing something, and settle in Alberta. The province was positively booming. Calgary boasted a population of 453,812 people, and houses were being built all over the place. The Husky Tower was about the tallest building in town, but that was about to change. We had never seen such construction, having come from a country where houses were almost all built with bricks. Those wood-framed houses were incredible; they were built so rapidly and so close together in massive subdivisions. And there were so many of them.

Nails—we had never imagined that so many nails could be used in construction, and so many were wasted. It seemed that the construction workers were in such a hurry, they did not bother to pick up the nails they dropped. Where did the nails come from? A long way off it seemed, but then everywhere is a long way off in such a huge country. Nobody was making them in Alberta, but apparently some outfit by the name of Irving Wire Products in Calgary used to make them. We did a little research and visited Harry Irving, who was most helpful. He advised us about what the best machines were and which ones to avoid, where we could locate some, and an idea of what we should pay for that equipment. He also agreed to supply us with wire drawn down to the different gauges we would need for the various lengths of nail that we were planning to make. We decided that manufacturing nails would be something that any old fool should be able to do and could be fun and profitable.

We located a used Wafios S110 nail machine in Connecticut that was costly but affordable. It was exactly the machine that Harry said would be best for our application, as it was capable of making a wide array of nails and was a well-made precision piece of equipment. His advice was excellent, and that first machine, although difficult to set up, turned out to be first rate and amazingly durable. I suspect you could run that machine all day, every day, for a hundred years and only replace a few bushings during the entire time. No wonder they don't make cars like that; they would last a lifetime, and that would not be good for business.

We had a reasonable amount of money, but the project was frighteningly capital intensive, and it would take a while before we could expect to have any income. We decided that our best approach would be to purchase some cheap land in a small town and put up our own building. Then we would have an asset that we could borrow against to give us the necessary working capital to get going.

Not only was cheap industrial land of vital importance but an affordable house to live in was also essential. We had checked out all sorts of places as diverse as Hillcrest Mines, Lundbreck, Fort Macleod, Claresholm, and Stavely. The going price for industrial land was around $3,000 an acre, and seeing that we wanted two acres, that was $6,000. It might not sound like much today, but back then it was enough to buy a basic half-ton truck brand new. We located a total of three houses that seemed adequate and affordable: one in Hillcrest Mines, one in Stavely, and the best one in Granum, which George Miller of Smith Agencies in Claresholm had shown us. Up until then, we had over-looked Granum, so we decided to take a closer look.

We drove to Granum and went straight to the bar in the Alberta Hotel and enquired as to who the mayor was. Ege Mohr was the reply, and a quick look in the phone book revealed his phone number. I called him right away on the pay phone in the bar, which cost ten cents at that time. As luck would have it, he picked up the phone. I told him that I was Edward Goodliffe, and I had recently ar-  rived from London, England, and was looking for some industrial land with the intention of establishing a nail factory.

"Where are you calling from?" he asked.

"The Alberta Hotel," I replied.

"I will be right down," he said.

A few minutes later, a pickup truck arrived and out stepped Ege Mohr, duly attired in cowboy hat and boots. This was not London! "Jump in my truck and I'll show you the industrial land," he said.

Granum was an imposing little town of 325 people with the library, post office, Save More grocery store, Alberta Treasury Branch Bank, and a fine-looking town office, fire hall, Standard garage, and UFA bulk fuel station all on the main street, with five imposing grain elevators on the other side of the railway track opposite the disused railway station.

Ege drove us north up Main Street and turned east over the railway track and then south down the road that went to the elevators. As we were driving along, we heard the history of Noble Blade, which had considered locating in Granum but had ended up in Nobleford and grown into a thriving business.

Just as we were passing the Willow Creek municipal grader shed and the entrance to the ball park, Ege announced that this was the industrial land. There were a couple of horses grazing but no sign of any industrial development.

"Not much going on here," we commented.

"No," said Ege, "we would really like you to locate in our town."

"How much for two acres?" we asked.

"How about six thousand dollars?" was his reply.

"Well, that is the same as Claresholm and the other towns locally. Can't you do better than that?" We explained our strategy of getting cheap land, putting up a building, and then borrowing against that asset to raise the necessary working capital to get us going.

He thought our plan had merit, and after a few minutes of deliberation, he said, "Why don't I just give you the land?"

"Wow, that's great, Ege. You've got a deal!"

A few moments later, he told us that maybe he was a bit ahead of himself, as he was only the mayor, and the council would have to approve the deal. We suggested that with his support, we felt sure we could sell the councillors on the idea, and we made arrangements to attend the council meeting a few days later.

Grant and I got straight to work, and after a few hours, with some big sheets of paper and a felt-tip pen, we had an impressive presentation worked out.

In phase one, we would construct a two-thousand-square-foot building on a one-foot-thick concrete pad. We would then construct an overhead hoist system for moving the wire carriers. At that point, we planned to install one nail machine and then a second a few months later. We planned to purchase wire drawn down to the various gauges we would require, and we would then make nails and sell them.

Somewhere down the road, we would go to phase two. At this point we would double the size of the building, extend the overhead hoist system, and install wire drawing equipment so we could buy wire rod directly from the steel mills at a greatly reduced cost and draw our own wire. We would install another nail machine, a nail tumbler, and a sophisticated packaging system.

It was a bold and impressive plan. A bit of a stretch maybe, especially when you consider that a basic wire drawing machine had a price tag of about $70,000 and required a massive amount of electrical capacity that Calgary Power quoted around $25,000 to install.

How on earth would we be able to make enough profit to cover that sort of expenditure? Ridiculous as it was, we even had a phase three in which we planned a further expansion. We were even going to go into the scrap metal reclamation business and melt down scrap steel and extrude our own wire rod.

Looking back to that day, it is incredible to consider that we actually managed to achieve phase two. Thanks to a fortuitous opportunity that came along, we were able to purchase the highly specialised equipment we needed at a tiny fraction of what it was really worth. I will get to that story later.

(3)

———∽∾∾———

A Hesitant Start

The first step was to put up a building, and it did not take us long to decide that a two-thousand-square-foot steel Butler building would be just fine for us. We ordered the package, and soon it arrived.

Larry De Maere, the local road grader operator, came straight over and leveled the ground for us in preparation for laying the concrete pad. We hired Allan Park from Fort Macleod to do the concrete, and we set the bolts ready for the frame to be secured.

I had absolutely no experience whatsoever with construction, but Grant knew a little from his work assisting a bricklayer in London, and also from working on the construction of the Victoria Line tunnel for the London Underground. Fortunately for us, the local people took a great interest in what we were doing, and there were plenty of advisors dropping by; they were a great assistance to us. Not thinking about the prevailing Chinook wind, we started to erect the east wall first. Doug Barnes was quick to point out that erecting the east wall first was a grave error. Fortunately we moved quickly and had the west wall completed as well before the wind picked up. Not only did Doug offer advice, but he also worked with us and refused to be paid. Chick Calderwood was the same and arrived with his backhoe. The front-end loader was invaluable for erecting the beams and lifting the insulation and steel sheets.  In short order, the building was up, the electricity and gas were connected, and it was ready for action.

We had located a used Wafios S110 nail machine in Connecticut and ordered it. The vendor had offered us the opportunity to view the machine, but we decided that we would not really know whether it was good or not, having never seen such a piece of equipment before, so we decided to save the cost of airfare and buy it unseen.

The nail machine arrived in Calgary and was held up at customs. They wanted to charge us a massive amount of duty, and our brokers thought they were wrong. Someone suggested that we should contact our member of Parliament, which we did right away. Ken Hurlburt came to the rescue. His family owned the gravel pit just north of Fort Macleod, and he was most agreeable and keen to help us. In next to no time, the machine was cleared with no duty to pay, and it was delivered to Granum.

Our excitement upon receiving the machine soon turned to disappointment when we realized that vital components were missing, which rendered the equipment inoperable. It seemed strange that they would sell a nail machine without a wire straightener, gripper dies, cutters, and a header die, but that was exactly the condition it arrived in. Having never seen one of these machines before, we had no idea what they even looked like, but it was obvious that certain parts were missing.

After examining the machine carefully and turning the flywheel by hand, we were able to figure out how it worked and what pieces were missing. Where could we possibly purchase the necessary dies? It soon became apparent that local machine shops in Lethbridge and Calgary did not have a clue about making what we needed. In desperation we called Wafios in Germany, and the company gave us the name of its representative in Canada. We contacted him and explained the situation. Apparently Wafios did not normally supply dies and cutters for its machines, as most nail manufacturers had their own die shops and would make their own. They helped us out by supplying ten gauge dies, a header, and some cutters. They also referred us to a fellow by the name of Norm Oliver who operated the Pittsburgh Carbide Die Company in Elizabeth, Pennsylvania, where we bought all of our dies from that point on. Norm was wonderful; he was obviously an independent diemaker who made precision dies for those nail makers who did not have their own die shops. His workmanship was superb, and his dies were considerably better made and more durable than the ones supplied by Wafios. As the dies wore out, we would send them back to Norm, and he would recondition them for a fraction of the original cost.

While we were waiting for the nail dies to arrive, we purchased a bright red 1966 Dodge 600 three-ton truck from Skip's trucks in Calgary and promptly hired Roger Smedstead of Claresholm to signwrite it with our name, logo, telephone number, and tare and gross weight limit. He did a great job, and it looked really professional

We also purchased a substantial arc welder, drill, and other tools so we could erect the overhead hoist system. We bought a one-ton, three-phase electric hoist from Kristian Electric in Calgary; commissioned Dominion Bridge in Calgary to bend some six-inch I beams to the shape we required; and proceeded to erect the track that went from the middle of the doors at the north end, around a corner to a few feet from the west wall, and then most of the way to the south end of the building.

As soon as we had that done, we picked up some ten-gauge wire from Irving Wire Products and took it to the factory. We bolted the

Wafio to the floor and had the seven-horsepower, three-phase, 220-volt motor wired in. The dies arrived, and we started on the biggest challenge of all: making a nail that actually resembled what it was supposed to be. There was no instruction manual. We had to figure it out by good, old-fashioned trial and error.

It was unbelievably frustrating. It seemed that there were so many adjustments, and every one would affect all of the others. The point could be off centre, so you would adjust it so it was straight, only to find that the head would then go off centre. On attempting to correct that, the head would get too thick or thin; then it would go up or down, to one side or the other. By the time it looked good, the point was off again. We would correct that, and the head would be too small again; then the points would not clear properly, or the nails were the wrong length or bent. It's funny to look back on it now because, over the years, I became so familiar with the machines that I knew precisely how to make all those adjustments. I feel certain that even today I

NAILED IT

would be able to fit the gripper dies, header die, and cutters and have the machine set up and ready to go in short order—and the nails would be perfect. Rather like riding a bicycle: once learned, never forgotten.

After several days of fighting the machine, we managed to get it to make a respectable-looking nail, so we went over to the Granum Town Office to tell them the good news and show them the first nails. There was great excitement at the town office, and one of the nails was promptly nailed into the wall in recognition of this momentous occasion. I remember that event so well, but for some reason, I cannot recall exactly where that nail was driven, which is such a shame because I would like to be able to go into the town office and point to the nail. With a few 3½-inch nails made and boxes on hand, we were ready to start limited production.

Having invited Ege Mohr and everyone around Granum to the official opening of the nail factory on October 8th, we went to the Claresholm, Fort Macleod, and Lethbridge newspapers and told them as well, hoping for some free publicity.

We held the opening in the early evening. Duly attired in our pinstripe suits, we welcomed a big crowd to the factory. Ege Mohr gave his speech and told everyone how proud he was to be officially opening the nail factory in Granum and what a milestone this was for the town. He had been trying for a long time to attract some industry, and at last, he had done it and wished us the best of luck. We told him that we were going to do our best to put Granum on the map.

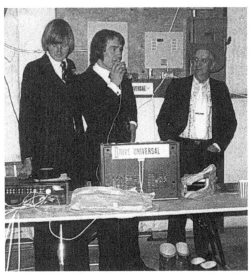

From the left Edward, Grant and Ege Mohr.

As Murphy said, "If anything can go wrong, it will." Well, it did right on cue. We had been careful to have the machine set up perfectly so it would produce good-quality nails at the opening ceremony. Ege pushed the start button, the belts squealed, and the machine was soon up to full speed. Three hundred and twenty-five nails a minute came pouring out of the production chute, and every last one of them had the points stuck. To add insult to injury, a big gob of grease flew off the main crank and landed right on Grant's suit.

Despite the malfunctioning of the machine, it was a most successful evening. There was a big, enthusiastic crowd wishing us well. I cannot remember everyone, but some of those in attendance included Ege and Elvina Mohr, Alan Munro, Kay Cairns, Lloyd and Kay Sherman, Tom and Linda Blair, Russell and Nellie Blair, Agnar Johnson, Sid Hoglund, George Miller, Marcel Pratte, Jack and Judy Hoglund, Doug Barnes, and Eleanor Rondeau. The coverage in the newspapers was better than we could possibly have hoped for with front page articles in both the *Claresholm Press* and the *Fort Macleod Gazette*. Even the *Lethbridge Herald* mentioned the opening in a short article.

(4)

BIRTH OF THE GRANUM GRIPPER

INVIGORATED BY THE newspaper publicity, we hit the road to find some customers. Not really knowing what sort of nails we should be making, we headed off to building sites to meet the people who were using the nails. We showed them our product and right away discovered that very few people were using 3½-inch nails because they were too long. A two by four stud of lumber was 1½ by 3½ inches. Three-and-a-quarter-inch nails were what they wanted.

We asked everyone what they did not like about the nails they were using and how we could make them better. Most framers were using phosphate-coated box nails, and for some reason they were made with paper-thin heads that easily broke off if anyone tried to pull them out. They did not like that, so we took note of it and made ours with thicker heads, which made them resistant to breaking off.

We had not realized that almost everyone was insistent on having phosphate-coated nails. We had not thought about that. Apparently, the coating made the nails grip in the wood, whereas the smooth, shiny nails tended to work their way out. We had to figure out how to phosphate-coat our nails. After a lot of phone calls, we found a chemical company that supplied us with a compound of phosphoric acid by the name of Granodraw that had to be diluted in hot water. The nails were immersed in the solution for about fif-

teen minutes and then rinsed and dried. We tested it out in a couple of oil drums, and it worked quite well.

We picked up some quarter-plate steel sheets and got to work welding a coating tank, and we had Marcel Pratte, the local plumber and gas fitter, equip it with gas burners and a chimney. We also welded a packing table where we planned to dry the nails and pack them into boxes. We located that table in front of a forced-air furnace that we had

Maurice Martin using the coating tank.

purchased from Jack Hoglund. It was a secondhand oil-burning furnace that had been converted to burn natural gas.

The acid tank seemed to work okay provided the nails were dried quickly enough. If they took too long to dry, they would turn red with rust. Blowing hot air onto the packing table took too long, so we looked for an alternative method and ended up purchasing a Sperry New Holland industrial spin dryer, and that worked perfectly. It thoroughly dried the nails in about five minutes.

NAILED IT

By this time our nails were beginning to get a reputation for not holding, and as we had finally perfected the phosphate-coating process, we needed to rebrand the nail with a name that indicated superior holding power. We called it the Granum Gripper, and from that point on, our boxes were printed with "Granum Grippers, manufactured by Universal Nail, Granum, Alberta" and our telephone number.

We were required to print everything in French as well as English, but we only had English on our boxes. One day the phone rang and the caller wanted to speak to the manager, so I said that was me. He was calling from Wandering River, and he proceeded to tell me how pleased he and his team of framers were with our nails. He then went on to say that they were particularly impressed that we had no French on our boxes. How did we get away it? The fact is, we had not even thought about it. We never did comply with the regulation.

Around that time, we unbolted the Wafios from the floor in the middle of the room and moved it to the southeast corner of the building. We raised it about a foot off the ground and bolted it onto four little stands that we made for it. Doing that enabled us to fit small oil drums under the production chute, and those drums had lots of holes in the bottom so the acid solution could flow into and out of them.

We also welded hooks on the top rim so we could use the overhead hoist. We could fill the drums under the nail machines, move them on a trolley to the acid tank, lift them with the overhead hoist into and out of the tank, and then into and out of the rinsing tank, and into the spin dryer; from there it was onto the packing table.

At that time, we received our second nail machine that we purchased from Bob Glader of the

Grant checking the Glader.

William Glader Machine Works in Chicago. It was a reconditioned Glader Number 2 nail machine and was the American-made equivalent of the Wafios S110. We set that up on stands right beside the Wafios.

We also took delivery of a wide selection of dies purchased from Norm Oliver and proceeded to make two-, 2½-, three-, 3¼-, 3½-, four-, and five-inch nails for stock.

Our initial sales effort was mainly concentrated in Lethbridge, as that was the closest city, and also towns close by such as Fort Macleod, Claresholm, and Pincher Creek. Some of the very first customers were John's Construction and Economy Lumber in Fort Macleod and Walter Stewart's Nu Mode Homes in Lethbridge.

Nail sales were increasing, and we were becoming better at making them. Looking back on the first few weeks of production, I realize that our nails were not very good at all, and those early customers helped us to perfect our nail.

As time went by, our quality became better and better to the point that I could rightly claim that the Granum Gripper was the best nail you could buy.

Our first employee was Les Anderson from Claresholm; we had met him when he worked for Beaver Lumber there.

Grant and I soon realized that we were not getting enough sales to become profitable. He was convinced that we needed to sell to wholesalers so we could reach the necessary volume that would enable us to get the cost per box low enough to make us profitable. I could see his line of reasoning, but the profit margin was going to be so slim, I was worried that we could easily slip into a loss-making situation. After much deliberation, we decided to go ahead and

Les Anderson

try to break into the wholesale market.

Our first wholesale customer was Advance Distributors in Lethbridge and Calgary. We dealt with Mel Ruston, and he was a very likable fellow. He paid promptly and was a pleasure to deal with. Of course, he was insistent that we should not sell to any retail customers, so we referred all our existing customers to him. They ordered fairly large quantities, but the margins were rather skimpy. Fairly soon after that, we managed to convince MacMillan Bloedel in Calgary and Edmonton to buy from us. We dealt with Wilkie Wanless in Calgary and Dennis Jeffares in Edmonton. Wilkie was an interesting man but a tough negotiator, and our margins were virtually nonexistent.

Granum had its share of characters, and around this time Grant and I went out to Clarence De Maere's home. Clarence was advanced in age and liked to drink a lot of alcohol. Grant had been talking to him at the Alberta Hotel bar in Granum, and there was something he had that he wanted us to pick up. I'm not sure what it was after all these years, but when we arrived at his farmhouse in the late afternoon and knocked on the door, we heard him shout out for us to come in. We entered the kitchen, and there was no sign of Clarence. He then shouted out again to inform us that he was in his bedroom and to come in. What a sight it was: there was Clarence lying in his bed with the covers over him, but he still had his cowboy boots on sticking out of the bottom of the bed. He was in the process of sobering up and clearly had not sufficiently recovered to get back on his feet.

His home was six miles east of Granum, and somehow he managed to drive home from the Alberta Hotel in an absolutely paralytic state on a regular basis. It was plain to see that Seagram's Five-Star Rye Whisky was his favorite, as the walls of his bedroom had scores of labels stuck to the paint.

While I am on the subject of Clarence, there is one more delightful story about him that I must relate. Some months later, we heard that Clarence was in the Fort Macleod hospital; apparently he was "drying out," according to the local gossip. Grant and I decided to make the fourteen-mile journey to Fort Macleod to visit him.

We arrived at precisely the right moment to witness an incredible sight: Clarence striding down the hallway without a stitch on. He informed us that he was going home. Apparently they had told him that he was in no fit state to leave, and he had replied that he was going anyway, so they refused to let him have his clothes. He said in that case he would go as he was, but they said that he could not take the hospital clothing either, so he had thrown it off in disgust and was leaving stark naked. And what a sight it was: Clarence, the original stick man. What a character!

We had a chat with the hospital staff and said that we would take him. They gave him his clothes, he signed himself out, and we took him home. The next day he was back to his normal routine at the Alberta Hotel bar.

I'm not sure when he died, but my son Justin and I dropped by his abandoned and very derelict farmhouse in 2014 and walked around inside.

It was a bit hazardous because the roof was full of holes as was the floor, and the windows were gone. A lot of the plaster had fallen off the walls, and in Clarence's bedroom, there was no sign of any of the Seagram's Five-Star labels, which was a shame as I was hoping they would still be there. Alas they were gone. What was there were the remains of Clarence's bed.

As I stepped outside and looked around, imagining the years that he had looked out at that  same magnificent view of the Porcupine Hills and snow-capped Rocky Mountains in the distance, I could not help but feel a wave of sadness that dear old Clarence was gone, and his house and outbuildings were being reclaimed by the windswept prairie.

(5)

Maynard's Quick Haircut

We were now getting orders for large quantities of nails, which required greater production, so we hired Maynard Dixon and Maurice Martin, as well as Les. The winter had arrived, and it was a cold morning. All five of us were in the factory getting everything ready to go. When Maynard tried to turn on the gas furnace to warm up the place, nothing happened, and he let us know there was a problem. Grant, Les, Maurice, and I were busy greasing machines, moving wire, assembling boxes, and getting the acid tank fired up, and I shouted to him to check the pilot light to see if it had gone out. He checked and, yes, it had gone out, so he proceeded to relight it.

As I mentioned earlier, it was an old piece of equipment that we had purchased from Jack Hoglund. It had been an oil-burning furnace and had been converted to natural gas. It was much cheaper than a new furnace, which is why we bought it. As it was an oil burner, there was a six-inch-wide inspection flap at head height when you crouched down to light the pilot. It must have been there so you could see into the combustion chamber when adjusting the oil flow to the burner.

Suddenly, there was a monumental explosion, the inspection flap opened up, and a huge sheet of flame engulfed Maynard and blew him onto his back. The force of the blast was so great that several feet of the chimney tore off the top of the furnace and went crashing to the floor. "Oh no, Maynard's dead!" We all rushed over, and he slowly got up from the floor in a rather stunned state, but other than a quick haircut and a blackened face, he was largely unscathed. Dear old Maynard looked a bit like a raccoon. He took it in his stride and burst into laughter, and we all joined him. Where his glasses had been, he had white circles around his eyes, and the rest of his face was black. His hair was so burned off, he only had about half an inch of hair left, and his eyebrows were totally gone.

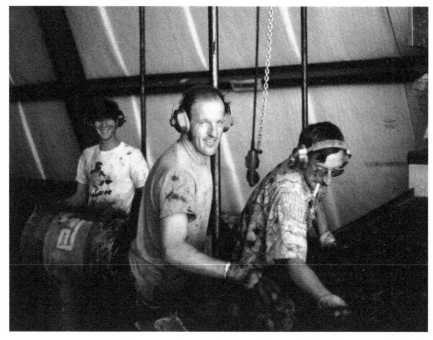

From the left: Les, Maurice and Maynard.

(6)

———◆———

ROLLING THE DICE

THE DECISION TO ramp up production and sell a large volume of nails via wholesalers was a significant gamble and necessitated a massive increase in our working capital.

We banked at the Alberta Treasury Branch in Granum. The manager at the time was Clare Websdale. He liked our strategy of getting the land and erecting the building in order to have a substantial asset to use as security to borrow money. He liked our business plan and recommended to his superiors that we should be financed. Fred Sparrow came down from the head office to check us out and gave the loan his approval. In fact, there was an article about us in the 1975–6 Treasury Branch annual report. We had the facility to borrow up to $70,000 on a revolving credit, and that was a lot of money in those days. Unfortunately, we had to personally guarantee the loan and pledge our house in Granum as security on top of the nail factory. I was most uncomfortable doing that, but without the working capital, we were dead in the water.

Many years later when the Canadian Western Bank started up, I noticed that Fred Sparrow was the president. I decided to drop in and see him and managed to get an appointment without any difficulty. I introduced myself and congratulated him on his new assignment, and I proceeded to let him know that our paths had crossed many years before when he was with the Alberta Treasury Branch. He could not place me, and so I asked if he remembered the Granum Gripper? His response was immediate; indeed he remembered and had thought that I looked very familiar. I said to him that if our roles had been reversed, I'm not too sure that I would have made that loan as it was ridiculously risky. I then asked him why he decided to authorize that massive loan. Without hesitation, he said that he felt sure we would be successful because we were so enthusiastic and determined that nothing would stop us achieving our objective. He went on to say, "You did pay off the loan, didn't you?" When I replied in the affirmative, he said, "I knew you would, well done."

By this stage, we had stopped buying our wire from Irving Wire Products largely because its wire was too soft, which made it very difficult to clear the points. The company was using a 10-10 carbon wire rod because it was ideal for making weld mesh, which was Irving's main product. We needed 10-15 carbon wire because it hardened more during the drawing process and made for stiffer nails, and the waste would break off the points of the nails more easily as the metal was more brittle. We were purchasing most of our wire from Terry Galbraith at Titan Steel of Surrey, British Columbia, and brought it to Granum in full twenty-ton truckloads, which was the most economical way to do it.

Soon, we had complaints that our boxes were too big and the nails were difficult to get out of the boxes because they were not packed neatly like our competitors' nails. We could not afford automated packaging equipment, so we did the next best thing: we ordered from England a 600-volt DC electromagnet specially designed to line up nails in our boxes. When it arrived, we set it up at the end of our packing table, and it worked incredibly well. We were able to reduce the size of our boxes by 40 percent, and the nails were so neatly packed that when you opened the boxes, the nails were perfectly lined up. Although it was expensive to buy, it did not take long to pay off the magnet with the savings in the cost of boxes.

The magnet at the foot of the packing table.

Sales increased as we picked up more customers. We even exported some nails when we sold to Barbara Hibbard of Georgia Pacific in Great Falls, Montana. By the autumn of 1976, it was becoming evident that despite the large volume of nails we were making and selling, we were not really making any profit. The wholesalers were incredibly slow at paying, but our suppliers expected to be paid promptly, and, of course, the men had to be paid on time.

Grant became less and less interested and put in fewer and fewer hours. I became very worried about the situation and did everything I could to keep our costs as low as possible and get the customers to pay as much as possible and as soon as possible. Grant felt burned out and told me that he needed a break; he was going back to England for a few weeks. He left and did not return for three months.

During the time he was away, Jane and I decided that if we continued on this course, it was going to bankrupt us. I went to our customers and explained to them that we simply could not continue to supply them at the current price. We needed a bit more, and we needed to be paid thirty days after delivery rather than the sixty to ninety days that they were currently taking. All of them refused my proposal, and within a few days, Universal Nail had no customers at all. It was a terrible situation to be in. We owed the bank a fortune, and at that point in time, we were absolutely stalled with no customers and three men on the payroll.

Drastic action was required. I laid off the three men and hit the road to sell our nails. The plan was to sell directly to building contractors anywhere within two hundred miles and to sell to wholesalers and lumberyards anywhere beyond that limit with a few exceptions.

I had hardly got started, and Grant returned. I explained to him the situation and what I had done to correct it. I proposed that I should buy him out. He agreed and left in February 1977. Being a man of great talent, Grant could see that computers were the wave of the future, and he decided to ride that wave. He joined IBM where he was being groomed as a system engineer. He found that incredibly boring, and he also disliked being in

Grant

Toronto, so he headed back west to Calgary where he was hired by Sperry Univac in system sales. He was in his element and did a magnificent job there. Altel Data, a division of AGT (Alberta Government Telephones) wanted to go into computer sales, and that is where Grant came in: Altel Data had no experience with computers, and Grant had carte blanche to do what he liked. He described the experience as "jolly good fun," and he built the business into the dominant player in Alberta. Having achieved that, he decided he wanted to go to the west coast and joined Tandem computers and then Wang computers as sales manager. He could see the end in sight for the mainframe computer industry and started the Genesis Group.

The first people I went to see were the original customers we had before we handed them over to the wholesalers. Most of them were happy to switch back to buying from us. Virtually every day I was out selling, and I kept picking up new customers, but I needed to get a lot of new customers right away.

(7)

GRANUM RADIO

GRANUM WAS A rather sleepy town of 325 people and a large portion of the population were retired farmers and ranchers; however, there were some young people, including three young men who had a rock and roll band by the name of Black Dawn—vocalist and lead guitar player Randy Munro, whose father was the Alberta Wheat Pool manager in town; bass guitar player and backup vocalist Wally

Wocknitz, and drummer Brian Perret, whose father was the manager of the Save More Store.

The band used to practice in Blunden Hall, but they were finding it rather costly to rent. I suggested that they could practice in the nail factory for free, and they did just that about once a week.

From the left: Brian Perret, Mrs Moneo, Stella Perret, Cliff Perret and Sheila Hahn.

Not much happened in Granum on the weekends, and I suggested to Brian that it might be fun to get a transmitter and broadcast to Granum for a few hours on the weekends. He thought it was a great idea, so I went to see Peter Hahn, who owned and operated a television and radio store in Claresholm. I did not know Peter before walking into his establishment that day, and I went up to him and asked if he could make me a transmitter.

He said, "What do you want, a citizens band radio?"

"No, I want an AM radio transmitter," I replied.

"That's illegal," he said.

"I'm not asking if it is legal; I'm asking if you can make me one."

He responded, "Well, yes, I can make you one. I can easily modify an old valve radio receiver and turn it into a transmitter. How powerful do you need it to be?"

I told him that I wanted it to be able to cover Granum and a few miles around the town, and I asked how much that would cost. He said he would make it for $40, and it would be ready in a week. I ordered it.

What an amazing contraption it was. At about six inches wide and about eighteen inches long, it was essentially an old valve radio that had been modified to transmit rather than receive. The valves, capacitors, resistors, and other components were mounted on a piece of wood. There were some knobs and a switch, a plastic baby bottle with wire wrapped around it, and a small light bulb. There was a socket where I could connect my amplifier to the transmitter, and there were outlets for a ground and another for an antenna.

Incidentally, I have donated it to the Granum Museum where it is on display. The museum is run with great enthusiasm by Lloyd Sherman's nephew Mike Sherman. He does a great job.

On the transmitter, there was a tuning adjustment for setting the frequency and another adjustment for setting the output power, which was quite sensitive. That was where the light bulb came in. The ideal setting was the point at which the bulb would flicker just dimly. If it did not light up at all, the signal would be weak in relation to the carrier, and there would be a lot of hissing. If it was too bright, the sound would be garbled.

We used to broadcast from our house on Gray Street and utilized the clothesline as the antenna, and it worked very well. In those days, most people still had clotheslines as not everyone had dryers. We set our frequency for 1400 because that was a nice quiet spot during the day, and our signal was very powerful for about two miles and then faded fairly rapidly. Apparently the output power of our transmitter was about fourteen watts. At Claresholm, which was ten miles north, you could pick up the signal, but it was weak. On a good day, it would go twenty miles. At night, it was only good for two miles as a Vancouver station (CFUN) would overwhelm our signal.

We had a lot of fun with Granum Radio. We had our own theme song and numerous jingles. Brian and I were the only regular announcers. We played predominantly rock and roll music and put on several comedy programs featuring local people. One featured Lloyd Sherman, a former mayor of the town, in which he won the Granum Spitting Competition, replete with truly disgusting sound effects that we managed to create using my reel-to-reel tape recorder and slowing down the playback. Lloyd was interviewed to find out how he was so talented at spitting, and he credited his skill to many years of practice chewing tobacco.

We had listeners phoning in with requests, comments, and announcements. It was difficult to know how many listeners we had.

Suffice it to say, quite a lot of Granum people would tune in when we were on the air. It was always playing in the Save More Store. Whenever we were switching on, we would phone a list of people, who would in turn phone their lists of people, who would phone more, In that way we managed to alert all the people who were regular listeners, and we could do it quickly.

Lots of listeners phoned in with requests for songs to be played and for announcements to be broadcast. Regular programming would include "What's On in Granum This Weekend," a spot where parties, bridal showers, weddings, and other activities were announced. All too often, there was very little going on, which was the main reason we were on the air in the first place.

One notable incident was when the new bank manager, Lloyd Lang, came to town. On the Monday when he started, I went into the bank, and the door to his office was open. I walked in and introduced myself and welcomed him to Granum. He said, "I know you." I responded, "How can you possibly know me?" He then went on to tell me that he had been listening to me on Granum Radio on the weekend and was most impressed that such a little town would have its own radio station. When I said that I was surprised that he had tuned in to us, he said that he found us right away because we were the most powerful station on the dial, and he found our program most entertaining.

Peter Hahn very much enjoyed Granum Radio and was tuned in most of the time we were on the air, despite the rather weak signal in Claresholm. A year or so later, he rectified that situation by giving us another much more substantial transmitter that he had made out of the guts of an old television. The new transmitter had an output power of about forty watts, and the reception in Claresholm was greatly improved. At Stavely, twenty miles away, it was a bit weak, but you could still get it.

In 1979 Jane and I sold our house in Granum and moved a few miles out of town (more on that later). Brian continued to run Granum Radio on his own for another year or so, and then he too moved away, and our radio station ceased to exist.

(8)

WHAT A MESS

How could I have got into such a mess? There I was at the start of 1977 owing the bank an absolute fortune and the men on the payroll, with utilities to pay and very little in the way of accounts receivable. As the saying goes "When the going gets tough, the tough get going." This was a sink-or-swim moment, and I was damned if I was going to sink; decisive action was required and right away before things got even worse.

I don't know when it was exactly, but maybe it was at that moment that Jane asked me, "Why is it that we seem to live our lives from one crisis to the next?" And I suppose the answer to that question was that we had chosen to create our own employment, and as a result there were no guarantees, no safety net. We were risk-takers and were at the mercy of the free market and the regulators that interfere with the free market. It was a bit of a rough ride at times, but we never suffered from boredom.

Drastic decisions were made and implemented. Just as soon as I had a reasonable amount of stock built up, the men were laid off, and for the next few months, I did everything myself. When bigger orders came in and I could not keep up, I employed part-time help.

Using part-time help presented yet more problems. They had to be trained and that took time. On top of that, because they were new to the job, they were unfamiliar with the work and prone to making mistakes.

The plan was to cut the overhead to the bone, and laying off the men sorted out the biggest expenditure after the cost of the wire. Getting the cost of the wire down was of paramount importance, but no easy solution was in sight. To draw our own wire would reduce our cost considerably, but the cost of a wire-drawing machine was about $70,000 so that was out of the question. All we could do was find another cheaper source of drawn wire. Over the coming months, we bought from Titan Steel of Surrey, British Columbia, and it was cheaper than Irving; the wire was also of better quality. The biggest problem, however, was that we had to buy in full truckloads to keep the cost of transportation at a tolerable level. Even finding a trucking company that would do the job for a reasonable price was a challenge. Fortunately, we found Herb Peterson, a small independent trucker who gave us great service and was a pleasure to deal with.

The next part of the plan was to increase retail sales. Now that we had lost all of our wholesale customers, we decided to bypass them, and while we were at it, we also decided to bypass most of the lumberyards and hardware stores so we could take their markup too. At that level, we reckoned we could compete effectively and make a respectable profit at the same time. Now, of course, the next hurdle to surmount was who could we target and how could we reach them?

Well, we decided that the building contractors were the people we needed to get, and the framing contractors would be the best target. An essential part of the recovery plan was to make sure that the bank had no clue about the precarious situation we were in. If they called our loan at that time, we would have been finished. Bank repayments were paid on time even if other important things had to be delayed.

I hit the road in my little Datsun pickup truck with a collection of the likely sizes of nails that I could sell and headed off looking for construction sites.  Anywhere building was going on I would stop and sell our nails. As before, Lethbridge was my first target area as it was only forty miles away, and then I went to Calgary, which was ninety miles away. I handed out samples for them to try, and I pointed out all of the features that made our nails better than any of the others. I also took note of what they told me they wanted, and with that feedback, I kept improving our nail until, without doubt, it was the best nail on the market. Our delivery was prompt, and we were competitive, selling for slightly less than the lumberyards. The contractors were getting a better product delivered to them promptly for slightly less than they were paying before, and we were managing to get paid much more promptly. That had to be a winning combination, and it was. But there was a concern.

I was spending so much time driving that I could not be everywhere I needed to be; there was only one of me. I could not afford to hire anyone, so I had to maximize my time by hitting my best target the hardest, and that meant going to Calgary. There were hundreds of wooden buildings going up in Calgary so I could keep right on selling, and I was picking up quite a lot of customers. However, driving up to Calgary and back each day was wasting about four hours a day and using lots of fuel, and I often had the wrong sizes of nails in the truck or could not carry enough boxes. I needed a base in Calgary.

Looking into the cost of renting an office with an attached warehouse was a bit of a shock. There was no way we could afford that, so I decided to try another approach and see if I could sublease part

NAILED IT

of someone else's office with a warehouse. I went to a likely area in southeastern Calgary and called on one place after another. After being turned down numerous times, I came across Ken Gislasen who had a business called Porta-Bote of Canada at 6560 Second Street SE, overlooking the Glenmore Trail just east of Maclin Ford Auto Body. Ken was most receptive to my suggestion. He was only using about half of

the warehouse, and there was a reception area, an office, and a small kitchenette leading to a washroom. We made a deal to split the rent, and I was able to use the reception area and half of the warehouse. He took my phone calls and dealt with any customers when I was away, and I did the same for him when I was there and he was out. Ken was a good bloke, and the arrangement worked very well for both of us.

Mentioning the fact that we were situated near Maclin Ford Auto Body shop reminds me of a funny moment. One day I was on the phone giving a customer directions to the office. Somehow my tongue got tied, and the words came out all wrong, and it sent me into uncontrollable laughter. I told him the address and to turn at "Facklin Maud Auto Botty."

To help with my sales campaign, I needed some promotion, but I could not afford to spend anything, so I did the next best thing: I went to the Calgary newspapers and told them that I was a small nail manufacturer taking on the giants in the industry. The editor at *The Albertan*, which later became the *Calgary Sun*, liked my story and gave me a nice big spread in the business section. The headline read, "Universal, the giant-fighter: Nails coming out our ears," and went on to describe how I had built up production and was busy breaking into the Calgary market. A few months later I managed to get an even better spread in the *Calgary Herald*. The headline was "Young entrepreneur keeps hammering away at nail market," with a big picture of me in front of stacks of boxes of my nails looking very determined as I grabbed a big handful of nails out of an open fifty-pound box. It was a great help, and lots of the people I was approaching had read about me in the papers.

The plan was working; the cash was coming in, and we were picking up customers at a steady pace and keeping them. We had been in business for two years, and we celebrated with a party in the nail factory; everyone in Granum was invited. Jane decorated a cake and prepared a spread of things to eat and drink, and a good crowd turned up. I gave a demonstration of the two machines and explained the production process. Mayor Ege Mohr gave a speech, saying how pleased he was with our progress and how we really were "putting Granum on the map." He wished us continued success and received rousing applause. Ege's program of building the commercial base of Granum had brought another business to town. Housebuilder Noel Rice was there that evening, and he had just started on a project to build several new houses on the east side of Granum. I'm glad to say, he was building them with Granum Grippers.

It was wonderful that people cared, and it was a great encouragement to us. Remembering exactly who was there that evening is difficult, but I did find this picture showing a small sample of the crowd. Almost every day I would see Tom Blair, as he ran the post office, and we would invariably discuss current world events; we were very much on the same wavelength. His wife, Linda, was there that evening as were his parents, Russell and Nellie, who were delightful people. Just recently I

     NAILED IT

went to visit Tom and Linda with my son Justin. I had not seen them for possibly twenty years or so, and we just picked up where we had left off. It might as well have been a week. Alan Munro was our neighbour on Gray Street; he ran the Alberta Wheat Pool elevator and was a very fine fellow. On the far right of the picture is Peter Tschetter, who was the boss at the Granum

Left to right: Noel and Kathy Rice, Tom Blair, Alan Munro, Jane, Linda Blair, Lloyd Sherman, Nellie Blair, Unknown, Peter Tschetter.

Hutterite Colony. He was a good customer, and we became firm friends over the years. He was very interested in history and world events, and we spent many hours conversing on those subjects. Invariably his house would steadily fill with family and neighbours and would be bursting at the seams. From his introduction to Jake and John Walter at the Springpoint Colony, a similar friendship has developed, and I always enjoy visiting them. There are a lot of very fine people at both Granum and Springpoint Colonies. I always carry a reminder of Springpoint with me as I have a magnificent leather wallet that was made for me with great care by Sam Walter.

(9)

A WONDERFUL COMPLAINT

THE PUSH WAS on to break into the Calgary market. Day after day I was going around to the building sites talking to anyone who would listen. At the sites where nobody was there, I would leave a sample of nails in a plastic bag, my card, and a large card with "Wanted" printed across the top.

One morning I was awakened at about five thirty by the sound of the telephone ringing. I answered, "Universal Nail, good morning." The caller told me how impressed he was that I was answering the phone at such an early hour, as he was expecting to leave a message on a machine. He told me that he

WANTED

THE GRANUM GRIPPER

Very Tough and Packaged in 50 Pound Boxes
UNIVERSAL NAIL LTD., GRANUM, ALBERTA
Telephones
GRANUM FACTORY: 687-3996 CALGARY OFFICE: 253-8922

was John Bilan from the Alberta Wheat Pool, and he had a complaint to make. He proceeded to tell me that he had purchased some 2½-inch Granum Grippers from Macmillan Bloedel, and they were useless. What was I going to do about it? I asked what the problem was, and he told me that they were bent and the points were off to one side. I told him that I would replace them with good nails right away. How many boxes did he have? He told me he had twenty, and I said I would change them immediately. He gave me the address of his warehouse in Calgary and asked me to call him when the job was done.

I checked my stock, and fortunately I had twenty boxes of two and a halfs. Right away I opened them up to make sure they were all right and then sealed them up again. After loading them into my pickup truck, I headed to John's warehouse. After dropping off the nails and picking up the bad ones, I asked to use the phone so I could speak to John. I called to let him know that the nails had been exchanged. He was most impressed that I moved so quickly. I asked if I could make an appointment to see him to discuss the possibility of supplying him with my nails, and he told me to come and see him the next day. On arriving back at the office, I opened up all the boxes to see how many had bad nails in them and was greatly relieved to find out that eighteen of the twenty boxes were up to standard, so I restapled them and put them back in stock and put the two bad boxes aside to sell as rejects.

The following day I headed off to see John Bilan. I would never have thought of trying to sell nails to the Wheat Pool, as I had no idea that they used so many nails. Thank goodness he had made his complaint. He explained that the nail they used in the greatest volume was a four-inch common nail, and they normally bought them from MacMillan Blodel. He said that he might buy from us but only if we would supply them for the same price or less. I asked what that price was, and he checked the last invoice and told me. I was so disappointed; they were buying at very nearly my cost price. There was no way I could sell them that cheaply, and I told him.

I asked where his men were working so I could have a look at the nail they were using to see if there was anything I could do. He reached into one of the drawers of his desk, gave me one of the nails, and suggested that I go to see his men who were building an elevator near Calgary. I thanked him for his time and left.

The nail he gave me was very thick and heavy, much heavier than my four-inch nails. I picked up a box of my nails from the office and drove out to the elevator they were building. I introduced myself to the foreman and explained the situation. I gave him some of our nails and asked if he could get his men to try them out to see what they were like. They tried them, and they were just fine. Although

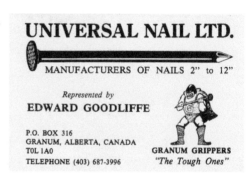

UNIVERSAL NAIL LTD.

MANUFACTURERS OF NAILS 2" to 12"

Represented by
EDWARD GOODLIFFE

P.O. BOX 316
GRANUM, ALBERTA, CANADA
T0L 1A0
TELEPHONE (403) 687-3996

GRANUM GRIPPERS
"The Tough Ones"

they were thinner, they did not bend and went in just the same. I asked whether they thought that the nails were any better or worse than the ones they were using. They said that they were just the same.

I explained that I needed their help, as I had to convince John Bilan to buy my nails. Would they write some positive comments on a piece of cardboard I picked up from the floor? "Okay," they said, "what do you want us to say?" My suggestion was "The Granum Gripper is a really good nail; it drives in easily and does not bend." One man commented and signed his name. Another wrote, "This is the best nail I have ever used," and signed his name. By the time I left, I had about eight very positive comments and their signatures on the piece of cardboard.

The men found it all very amusing, and I left with my piece of cardboard and a couple handfuls of the nails they were using. On returning to the office, I weighed a pound of their nails and counted how many nails there were. I did the same with mine and was delighted to discover that with my nails there were quite a few more in a pound. I calculated the cost per nail and discovered that if I charged four dollars extra per box for my nails than they were currently paying, they would actually pay slightly less per nail for mine.

I called John Bilan and let him know that I had good news, could I come and visit him. He said that would be fine and to come on over. When I got there, I showed him my nails, and then I showed him the piece of cardboard with all the comments on it. He put on his glasses and had a look at the comments. Within seconds he burst into laughter. "Oh come on, this is preposterous! Your nails can't possibly be that much better."

He picked up the phone and called the field office at the construction site and, after a bit of a delay, managed to speak to the foreman. I'm not sure what they said, but there was a lot of laughing. When he hung up, he said to me, "Those comments are hilarious. My men really liked you, and they actually said that your nails were just as good as the ones they were using, and that's good enough for me. Now, what are we going to do about the price?"

I explained that if I charged him four dollars more than he was currently paying per box, the cost per nail would be slightly less than the current price, and I would be able to make a profit. He called his assistant who located a small weigh scale, and I showed him what I was talking about. After seeing that, he told me he could live with that and asked his assistant to bring in the purchase order book, as he was going to try us out with a small order. When he handed me the order, I could hardly believe my eyes: he was buying twenty tons. That was the start of a long and profitable relationship, and it all came about because of a complaint.

(10)

WEDDING BELLS

IN JULY 1977, Jane and I got married in a little church in Claresholm. It was a blisteringly hot day, and the church was packed. My father, Tom, and Jane's mother, Edna, had flown out for the event and were staying with us in our rather small house on Gray Street in Granum.

No other family or friends from Britain came, but the substantial turnout of local people that filled the church was a great testament to how friendly and accepting the population of Granum and the surrounding area were to us strangers from afar. Local farmer Doug Barnes was my best man, and he drove us to the church in our old Mercury Montcalm, which looked particularly respectable that day—and thank goodness for the air-conditioning. Our dear neighbour on Gray Street, Lloyd Sherman, who was a very fine fellow, a

Lloyd with Jane.

retired farmer, and former mayor of Granum, gave Jane away.

The reception dinner was at the Scarlet & Gold Restaurant in Fort Macleod, where Chick Calderwood was master of ceremonies. He did an outstanding job and had everyone laughing.

After that, we had the evening dance at the Blunden Hall in Granum where the town's rock band, Black Dawn, supplied the music. My father had told me that he probably would not stay long, as rock music was not too much to his liking. As it turned out, he stayed right until the end and had a wonderful time, as everyone made such a fuss over him, and we had plenty of gin and tonic on hand, his favorite drink.

In the few days that he and Jane's mother spent with us, we were kept busy with lots of social engagements, and my father commented that he was astounded at how much the local people had accepted us. One thing was for sure, everybody loved him, and all the stories he told had them rolling in the aisles laughing; they had never met anyone quite like him.

While he and Edna were with us, it just so happened that Prince Charles was being made an honorary Indian chief at Standoff, which

Tom Goodliffe in the Dodge.

was not far from Granum, so we took them to the event.

When the day arrived for me to take my father to the airport, I had a large shipment of nails that needed to go to Calgary, so I drove him the 120-mile journey to the airport in the Dodge three-ton truck. That was the last day I ever spent with him, and in the last picture of us together, we were standing by that truck outside the Calgary office. A few months later he was dead. Dad was  fifty years old when I was born, so there was a big generation gap between us. He told me that he was proud of what I had done, taking the initiative to leave England and set up the nail factory in Alberta. Those few days together were the first and last time that we really connected, and that was maybe the first time in my life that I realized that you really have to savour every moment because you may not get another chance.

(11)

———— ⌇⌇⌇ ————

STAYING THE COURSE

THE PLAN WAS working, but it was taking a long time. For every two steps forward, I seemed to take one step back. Just as I thought that by cutting out the wholesalers and lumberyards, I could take the lion's share of the contractor market, I increasingly found myself up against Hillhurst Hardware. It was a hardware store in the north part of Calgary that targeted contractors, and it seemed to be prepared to use nails as a lost leader to keep the contractors coming back to buy saws, ladders, scaffolding, and anything else that would be profitable. Their selling price was essentially the same as Macmillan Bloedel, which was the hardware store's supplier. Presumably because of the huge volume Hillhurst sold, it must have been getting a special deal that enabled the store to sell at the price at which its competitors were buying. Although I could make a small profit if I sold at their price, it was not enough. There was a huge loan to pay off, and I needed capital to enable me to go to the next stage.

What could I do? It was quite a dilemma, and I ended up doing something that I was most uncomfortable about: I matched the price.

The reason I felt uncomfortable about it was that the loyal customers I already had were paying several dollars more per box, so they were effectively being punished for being my loyal customers, and I did not like that. I had no choice; it was the law of the jungle out there. I had to fight for market share and increase my volume of sales so I could get the cost per unit down.

To illustrate that point, imagine having a daily fixed overhead of $1,000. If I made ten boxes that would mean that I would have a fixed overhead cost per box of one hundred dollars, but if I made one hundred boxes, the fixed overhead per box would be ten dollars, which would be a whole lot better. It took me a few more years to figure out how to keep my profit margin and get the volume up at the same time.

With some of the low-price customers, I managed to get more from them when they found out that my product was better and they found value in my delivery service. Some of them would slip back into picking up their nails from Hillhurst, so there was no point in pursuing those people anymore. You can't win them all.

During 1978 I was able to ease off a bit as business was going all right, and there was actually some time to do other things. Jane and I liked gardening, but although our house on Gray Street was on a lot and a half, there was a big hedge around the backyard and several trees that tended to suck all the moisture out of our little vegetable patch. Also, when we watered the garden, it must have been hard on the plants because of the excessive amount of chlorine in the water; it smelled like swimming pool water.

Sid Hoglund ran the town water purification plant. The water was pumped a mile or so from Willow Creek to the filtration plant on the west side of town. Sid gave me a tour of the place one day. He was such a nice fellow, always cheerful, and he just about always was smoking one of those little cigars with the plastic holders on them. I asked him why the chlorine content of the water seemed to vary so much. He explained the process: After the water had been through the various filters, there was this mixing pool where he would throw in the odd shovelful of sodium hypochlorite. Apparently, he guessed the amount to put in, and if the creek was flooding he did not like the look or smell of the water, he would throw in a bit more for good measure. Nobody seemed to get sick, so I suppose old Sid knew what he was doing.

Jane and I had become good friends with Chick and Linda Calderwood, who lived about 150 yards away from us in Granum. Chick had a big spread of land and kept a huge herd of cattle. When we told him about the problems we were having with our vegetable patch, he offered to let us grow vegetables on a piece of land he had adjacent to Willow Creek. He even dug up the ground for us. We had great fun down there growing vegetables and swimming in the creek. We pumped water onto the garden, and things grew well, but we had not thought about the deer. As fast as the vegetables grew, the deer trimmed them off. It was a total failure but fun all the same.

That same year, we also had a great time with a Honda XL350 dual-purpose motorcycle that I bought secondhand. It was street legal but was also made for off-road riding. We went on a few camping trips where we drove up into the Livingstone Range of the Rockies west of Granum and the other side of the Porcupine Hills across Happy Valley.

We strapped on a tent and camping supplies and rode up the logging trails, managing to get up near the top of the mountain range. We camped up there, and it was absolutely wonderful. There were thousands of alpine flowers blooming in the meadows between little creeks with clear rushing water and magnificent views wherever we looked. Being at such a high altitude, the night sky was spectacular with many more stars visible than at lower altitudes.

It was probably crazy of us to camp there, but we survived and did not get mauled by the grizzly bears or eaten by the cougars.

I remember us visiting the Raspberry Ridge ranger station at the top of a mountain peak. We stopped to have a chat with the bloke running the place, and he gave us a tour. The lookout room had big windows all around. The roof of the building was bristling with lightning conductors connected to thick copper wires that ran off in all directions down the mountainsides. He told us how exciting it was during thunderstorms, as the building would continually get hit, and how effectively the conductors worked.

About a year later, the Alberta government decided it would deny people like us access to those high mountain trails and sent in bulldozers to destroy the access trails. That is just one of the many freedoms that have been lost over the years. How lucky we were to have had that incredible experience.

When I had big deliveries to make, I would use the Dodge 600. At full capacity, it could carry 288 fifty-pound boxes. One very memorable day, I was heading to Calgary with about one hundred boxes on board, and by the time I reached Parkland, the motor was misfiring so badly that I decided to pull into the village, and it died. I walked to the Alberta Wheat Pool elevator and asked if I could use the telephone. I called Willard Henker in Claresholm and asked if he could come and rescue me. Now Willard was quite a character; he ran Henker Motors, a Datsun dealership, with his sons. He soon arrived with a one-ton truck and a twenty-foot chain. He hooked it on to my Dodge, and off we went. Now anyone who has used a chain to tow a vehicle knows that there is no give at all, and when the chain goes slack and then tightens up again, there is a violent jerk that takes place. I can't imagine what was going on in old Willard's head, but he took off like a bat out of hell, and in no time we were going about seventy miles per hour. Obviously, he had not thought about the fact that my brakes were vacuum assisted, so they would not work properly without the engine running; and secondly, my vehicle weighing over seven tons and hurtling along at seventy miles an hour could not possibly pull up in less than twenty feet if there was an emergency. If someone had pulled out in front of him and he had to put on the brakes, I would have crashed right into him. I had absolutely no chance of stopping in less than a quarter of a mile. Talk about white-knuckle driving; I must have sweated a pint on that journey. All I could think about was Willard putting on the brakes and me running right over him. What a relief it was when we got there in one piece. Willard was totally oblivious to the extreme danger he had been in.

As time went by, I kept getting substantial orders for nails from John Bilan at the Alberta Wheat Pool. He had become a great supporter of Universal Nail and genuinely wanted to see us succeed. I had pointed out to him that it was unnecessary for him to order full twenty-ton loads. It would be better if he ordered 14,400 pounds at a time, which was 288 boxes. That worked out to six pallets with forty-eight boxes on each, and that was a full load for the Dodge, which I could then deliver. Each time he placed an order, he would ask what the price was, and I would say that it was the same as the last time. Invariably, he would say, "You can't charge the same price as last time; your costs must be going up, and I will pay you an extra dollar per box." His generosity was incredibly helpful and greatly accelerated the pay down of our business loan.

Each time I delivered to the Wheat Pool warehouse a very agreeable young man by the name of Greg Tetz was the forklift operator. During the unloading process, I would always have a good chat with Greg. As the months went by, Greg became more and more frustrated that he was stuck operating a forklift when really he wanted to work in the purchasing department in the Calgary city centre.

Periodically, I would take John Bilan out to lunch, which was most enjoyable. He was always very interested to hear about the adventures we were having, and there were always plenty of them to tell him about. I mentioned that I had talked to a very good young man by the name of Greg who was operating the forklift at the warehouse. His talents were being wasted, as he really wanted to have the opportunity to work in the purchasing office. Could he please consider him next time there was an opening?

A few months later, when I went to John's office to pick him up for lunch, I saw Greg at a desk in the main office, so I went over to have a chat. He was so excited to tell me that he had been so lucky. John had dropped by the warehouse and had talked with him, and that conversation had resulted in him being transferred to the office. His prayers had been answered.

(12)

THE OLD BRICK HOUSE

BY 1979, THINGS were running more smoothly. I had a good customer base in Calgary and Lethbridge, and I had picked up quite a few customers in Red Deer. In Calgary Ken Gislasen had closed down his Porta-Bote business, and I had taken over renting the office. To keep my rent down, I managed to sub-rent Ken's half to John Dale from High River, who ran a construction business, for two-thirds of the total rent. It was a good arrangement, and it worked well. I covered for him when he was out, and he handled things for me when I was out.

During 1976, Grant had for a short time rented a wonderful, old, three-storey brick house, seven miles east of Granum. The house had been built in 1917, and it belonged to Harold Stephenson. Harold had been left the house and farm for his life, and when he died, it was to be split amongst his siblings.

In 1979, Harold died, and the farm was sold off. Maurice Matheson bought it, and I think it came with a half section of land. Because Harold only had a lifetime interest in the house, he had done virtually no maintenance, and as a result, the place was virtually derelict. The basement and foundation were collapsing due to the sodium sulphate in the ground breaking down the concrete. This caused huge cracks to form in the brickwork. The cedar roof shingles were the original ones installed in 1917 and were in terrible shape. Inside, the plaster was cracked and falling off in places. Most people considered the house to be unfit to live in.

Edward and Jane.

As soon as Jane and I heard that Maurice had bought the place, we went to see if he would consider selling it to us. He told us that he was born there and would like to see the place restored. He had offered it to his sons, and neither of them wanted it because it was in such poor shape, so he made a deal with us. We paid him $30,000 for the house, outbuildings, and ten acres around it. That helped him pay for a fair bit of the land he purchased, and it was wonderful for us to have the chance to move out of Granum and have a potentially wonderful house. We sold our house in Granum for enough to buy the place for cash and have money left over.

That house was a dream come true, and we set to work right away re-building and repairing everything. The foundation was collapsing as I have already mentioned. We carried out thousands of pails full of concrete that had dissolved into gravel, as the only access was up some steps to a regular-sized door on the north side of the building. After setting up forms inside the basement and around the outside, we poured a new foundation with sodium sulphate-resistant concrete. It was a major undertaking and worked perfectly.

Jane was pregnant with Justin, and he was born in November. She loves to tell everyone how poor Justin spent his first days in "the ice palace," as at first we did struggle a bit to get the heating system up and running properly.

For the first year, we lived in a construction site. We hired experts to do the difficult things, and we did everything else ourselves to keep the cost at a manageable level. We insulated the walls by having holes drilled at the top of the walls and having cellulose insulation blown into the cavity between the lath and the outer wall. We filled the attic

with fiberglass insulation, installed new plasterboard everywhere that the plaster and lath had come apart, installed carpet and linoleum, and upgraded the bathroom, toilets, and the kitchen. We painted everything, hung lots of wallpaper, and replaced many of the light fittings. Outside we put on a new roof and had a bricklayer repair the brickwork. We painted all the wooden trim on the eaves and the window frames.

By the time we had finished, it was back to its original splendour, and what a magnificent house it was. I erected a flagpole outside our bedroom window and used to fly a nine-foot-long flag that was clearly visible from the secondary highway to Fort Macleod, half a mile to the east across the wheat field.

Now we had plenty of room for a vegetable garden, and we proceeded to grow large quantities of all sorts of fruits and vegetables. We froze enough corn, peas, beans, and other vegetables to keep us going through the winter, as well as storing lots of potatoes, carrots, and parsnips.

On the property there was the original house, which had at one time been the "Jumbo Valley" post office, as well as an old barn, a chicken house, a dilapidated garage, a shed, and some old wooden grain bins. We wasted no time and soon had chickens, sheep, goats, ducks, geese, and even our own Guernsey milk cow, Betsy. She was a very silly cow and a great expert at lifting her back leg up and sticking her hoof into the milk if she got half a chance. Normally, I was quick enough to move the bucket out of the way, but I do remember her scoring a

Justin and Robert with Betsy.

direct hit one day and being sufficiently infuriated that I got back at her by emptying the dirty milk over her head. Having lots of our own butter, cream, and milk was great.

In a small town like Granum, there are no secrets. Everyone knows what you are up to, so the word soon spread that we had bought the old Stephenson house and were renovating it. When it was built in 1917, it was one of the finest houses for miles around, and as we were restoring it to its former splendour, we had an endless stream of local people who wanted to have a tour, and we enjoyed showing them around.

Having all of those animals, we soon discovered that ten acres of land was not enough for us to grow all the hay we needed, so we looked for more land. The *Fort Macleod Gazette* advertised some for sale ten miles north of Fort Macleod, so I called the agent. It turned out that it was not north of Fort Macleod but a long way west of Fort Macleod in the Porcupine Hills, and we ended up buying it and putting up a little cabin. It was a piece of heaven up there, and we so enjoyed the place. During the summer it was a giant flower garden.

Thinking back to those days brings into focus so many freedoms we took for granted that have been taken away from us by busybody collectivist governments that want to micromanage our lives. They take away those freedoms all the while claiming that they are making things better. Nobody ever stands up for individualism and limited government. The solution to any problem is always a bigger, more powerful government, and invariably the more power that the government has, the less freedom that is left for the individual. It seems that governments at all levels get bigger every year, and if the trend continues, the total enslavement of the individual is assured. It is just a matter of time.

We were engaging in a massive rebuilding program with the house, and because we owned the place, it was totally our business what we did with it. Today, that would not be the case. We would have to pay for permits, and everything would have to be inspected. It would all have to be done "according to code." Anything not specified in the code would not be allowed, and the end result would have been that it would have cost too much for us to have contemplated, and that wonderful piece of antiquity would have just rotted away.

At that time there was a very innovative, thrifty, and industrious man who bought a small piece of land just west of the Dutch Reformed church on the Granum-to-Nobleford road, not far from the brick house. His name was Fred Shimpf, and he did not appear to be a wealthy man, but I suspect he was not short of a few dollars. He had managed to buy that small piece of land, and he wanted a home for his family. Over the course of a year or so, he managed to build a fairly respectable dwelling almost entirely out of discarded material he had scavenged from the municipal dump and from neighbours with old buildings that were being demolished. It was a wonder to behold, and I was most impressed with how he had done such a good job of very nearly creating a silk purse out of a sow's ear.

By hard work and dedication, that man with very limited resources had managed to build his own home. In today's world, behaviour like that is not tolerated, and he would not be allowed to have that house; the "authorities" would consider it unsafe and unfit for human habitation. Compared with what the early settlers had to endure, his house would have been quite luxurious. Why should people like him be denied the pleasure and satisfaction of building their own homes on their own piece of land just because they don't have pots of money or they don't want to be told how they must do the job? Collectivism stinks.

People need to wake up to what is happening. The freedoms are taken away incrementally; just a little bit here and a little bit there so nobody really notices. Everyone is too busy working to pay their ever-growing bills, and when they are not doing that, there is always the distraction of sport, alcohol, and drugs.

Today, if someone attempted to do what Fred did, they would be shut down immediately. With all the regulations in place, everything has to be built according to code, and that means that everything will be so expensive that only those with lots of money or lots of creditworthiness have a chance to build a house. This, of course, ensures that most people end up as debt slaves to the banks. They tell us that slavery was abolished, but really, it just changed its form, and it is getting worse with each passing year.

To the casual observer, the enforcement of these high standards appears to be making our communities so respectable. Everywhere you

look, people have beautiful new houses, and they are driving shiny new cars and trucks. The bureaucrats have managed to force a higher standard of living on everyone. Isn't that wonderful? Well, as we all know, nothing comes without a cost, and the price is much higher than it appears.

The way it was before the government interfered in the marketplace was much better. Yes, the houses were not so fancy and the motor vehicles were more basic, but many more people actually owned their own homes and motor vehicles. Today most homes and vehicles are owned by the banks, and people are struggling to keep up with the payments. It is great for the banks; they are sucking more lifeblood out of the economy than ever.

As well as individuals, governments at all levels are carrying record-breaking levels of debt, adding still more to the wealth being siphoned off by the parasitic banking system. While governments are spending more than they have coming in from taxes, there is the false appearance of prosperity, but it is an illusion. That debt has to be repaid, and it can't be.

The parasitic banking system that our entire civilization is built upon is such a fraud of truly monumental proportions, it is hard to believe that the conspirators have managed to get away with enslaving humanity the way they have. The banking system affects everyone, and yet it is not taught at school. Why is that? Even people employed by banks have no idea how it works. How can that be? It is nothing short of the most dastardly conspiracy for human enslavement ever devised. What a crying shame it is that the elephant in the living room goes unnoticed while so many lives are degraded by the existence of that elephant.

Maybe it is an unrealistic dream, but if a critical mass of people actually understood what was happening, this whole wicked control system of oppression could be replaced with sound money. In order to solve a problem, you have to understand that there is a problem, clearly identify it, and then find and implement a solution. My recommendation is that everyone needs to start by reading one particular book, *The Creature from Jekyll Island* by G. Edward Griffin. It is all about banking and the privately owned Federal Reserve Bank, which is not federal; nor are there any reserves.

When I came across this book, I thought that I needed to learn about this vital subject and was fully expecting it to be boring in the extreme. I was in for a shock; it turned out to be a rivetingly interesting look at history through the eyes of banking, and what a wicked tale of intrigue and deception it was. Read the book, and your perception of the world will never be the same again.

(13)

———— ❧ ————

NATIONAL ENERGY PROGRAM

THINGS WERE GOING fairly well, and we were enjoying renovating the house and growing our own food. Little did we know that Pierre Trudeau and his liberal government were about to deliberately devastate the Alberta economy. It was 1980, and Marc Lalonde introduced the National Energy Program. It sucked billions of dollars out of the Alberta economy, and the effect was instant.

Immediately after the announcement, the phone went dead. Sales dropped by about 90 percent the following month. The Alberta Wheat Pool, which normally purchased about sixty tons of nails a year, bought nothing for twelve months. Qualico Developments, which always bought a ton or more a month, purchased about one ton for the rest of the year. It was unlike anything I had ever experienced. I had to go back to the old program of laying off the employees and doing everything myself. It was like we were in a big game of snakes and ladders. From the beginning we had gone up a few small ladders and one big one when we got the free land. We had gone down a few small snakes, but this was a huge snake, and it had taken us right back. It was as if we had no customers; there were very few orders coming in.

Being in a situation like that tends to focus the mind a bit and cause you to redouble your effort. I embarked on a major sales campaign and also looked for specialty customers. I discovered that some electrical contractors put wall plugs in with nails rather than screws, and as a result I managed to pick up a few as regular customers. Harpat Industries, run by Ben Ostrander, made wooden plugs used in the oil industry, and he became a regular customer for three-inch nails. I also came across R & R Lumber at Frank in the Crowsnest Pass, which manufactured giant wooden reels used for coiling electrical cable, plas-

tic tubing, and rope. Its factory was at the foot of the famous rockslide where one third of Turtle Mountain had collapsed back in 1903, burying part of the town.

Amazingly enough, Lloyd and Kay Sherman, who we had lived next door to in Granum, told us how Kay's father was the guard on the first train to reach the slide on the morning it happened. Fortunately, someone had run up the track far enough to warn the driver to stop the train so it did not crash into the rocks that had buried the track.

The owner of R & R Lumber, Dick Koentges, had purchased a substantial British-made nailing machine that would drive a large number of nails all at the same time through the lumber and bend the tips over so they could not work loose. It was an incredible machine, but poor old Lud Margetak, the shop foreman, was having a terrible time trying to make it work properly because none of the nails available fit the machine properly, and it kept jamming up. Lud gave me the exact specifications the machine required for each particular job they had, and I made the nails accordingly. From that moment on, the machine did not miss a beat, and the productivity of the plant took off. Reels were coming off the production line like popcorn. What an incredible piece of equipment that was when it had the right nails.

Dick became a very good customer, but he was rather demanding and had a terrible habit of phoning on a Friday afternoon to place a rush order that he absolutely had to have on Monday. Thus I would have to work over the weekend when I would have preferred to be doing other things. His orders required me to change dies and completely reset a nail machine to make that specific nail. That process would take at least an hour or maybe two to get the nail perfect. Production would then start at 325 nails per minute. That would make a fifty-pound box in about fifteen minutes if it was a 3¼-inch nail. If it was a two-inch nail, it would take about an hour to make the same fifty-pound box. To keep busy while I was filling his orders, I would make other nails to build up my stock of the fast-moving sizes.

At first, I charged Dick approximately the same as he would have paid for regular nails. When I could see that my nails had enabled him to increase his production significantly, I asked for more. He made quite a fuss, but I got my increase. It was a great relationship; I made him exactly the nails he needed when he needed them. His nailing machine worked perfectly, and as time went by, he was able to give me advance notice, which enabled me to stockpile the nails so I did not have to work so many weekends.

When I had a heavy workload in the factory, Jane would deliver the nails, and unlike when I delivered them, she did not have to worry about unloading them because the men would rush straight over and do all the lifting. The men working there were a cheerful and friendly bunch. I remember swapping some boxes of reject nails with Terry Mikalski for a goat. I think he got the best of the deal, as she was rather grumpy and prone to butting the poor old sheep. Milking her was a challenge because she had one normal tit and the other one was so enormous, it was difficult to get hold of. She also managed to eat the tail off Jane's horse. What a goat!

As the nail factory was just across the road from the United Grain Growers elevator, I used to drop in to see the manager, Dan Kress, on a regular basis. Now that we were keeping chickens, I asked Dan if I could clean up the piles of grain that got spilled on the railway track while they were loading rail cars, and he said that was just fine. From then on, we had a plentiful supply of wheat and barley, which was absolutely wonderful. We built up a sizable collection of old breeds of chickens, including Speckled Sussex, Dorkings, Rhode Island Reds, Silver Laced Wyandottes, Cornish, Jersey Giants, and Old English Game, and we let them run all over the place. They were great fun to keep.

Naturally, there were some real characters amongst them, and some of the names still come to mind: JR, who was a bit of a bad boy; Mrs. Rippy, who spent a lot of time with almost no feathers for some reason; and of course, Mrs. Absolute Bastard, who truly lived up to her name by viciously attacking anyone who tried to take any eggs she might have been sitting on.

At times the egg production was prolific, and no matter how many there were, we always managed to sell them to our nail customers.

Looking back, I realize that it really was quite a challenge to satisfy all of our customers; they each had certain characteristics that had to be handled slightly differently. I suppose the reason I had some of them was because other suppliers were not prepared to make them feel appreciated, and I was. There was one customer who was all but impossible to completely satisfy, and I went to extraordinary lengths to keep his business.

He regularly bought a lot of nails and insisted on having a low price, so my margin was a bit skinny. Each time I delivered, there was always some little thing that he would complain about. Things like he had found a few nails without heads, or there were a handful of metal chips in a box, or the odd nail was bent. I came to the conclusion that the only thing that would satisfy him was to give him some free nails. Seeing that he had already managed to get my price down so low that I was not making very much, I was not prepared to give away any more, so I came up with a rather devious plan.

Roy was packaging 3¼-inch nails one day, and I instructed him to package forty-one boxes at one pound, five ounces light and put them aside. Removing such a small amount from each box was totally imperceptible, and the amount of nails removed was enough to fill another box.

When I made my next delivery, and he ordered forty boxes as I had anticipated, I told my customer how sorry I was that he had been inconvenienced by the things he had been complaining about. To put matters right, I was giving him an extra box at no charge.

The plan worked perfectly. He was so pleased with his extra box, and really I did not give him anything. He remained a loyal customer until the day we closed down.

By 1981 business was getting back to normal, and it was becoming apparent that pneumatic nailing guns were increasingly being used. I realized that I had better look into it and see if I could make collated nails for nail guns. The more I looked into it, the more daunting the project appeared. There were several different designs, and it seemed that each different brand of gun required a nail that would only fit that gun.

I forget exactly how I met Ken Gall, but he had worked for Sidbec-Dosco, a nail manufacturer in Quebec, for many years, and he had decided that he wanted to get into the manufacture of collated nails for use in nail guns. He proposed working with me to figure out how to do it. We would share the development cost and share the profit on all collated nails that we would subsequently sell. It was a good deal for both of us, as I already had the overhead covered by the existing sales so he did not have to worry about that. He did not know how to do it, and I agreed to work with him in the pursuit of uncovering that secret.

Craig Nicholson also joined in on the project. Ken managed to get our Wafios S110 to make nails with a D-shaped head, and we constructed various pieces of experimental equipment with which we tried to get them lined up correctly so they could be glued into strips. I had to keep the existing business going at the same time as this was all going on, so Ken and Craig put a lot more time into the project than I did.

All of a sudden, one Monday morning, Ken and Craig did not show up, and some of the experimental equipment was gone. Shortly thereafter, Ken advised me that he and Craig had figured out how to do it. He had decided that because he had figured out how to collate the nails, he did not see why he should share the profits that would result from his efforts with me when he did not need me anymore. He said he was going to establish a business with his girlfriend instead. They were going to buy a brand-new Wafios nail machine and set up their business in Fort Macleod, fourteen miles south of Granum.

What a shame that was. The essence of a good deal is where both parties gain from the project, and with the original plan, I thought we had precisely that. To get into production and secure enough sales to cover the overhead would obviously take several months at best, and during that time, the existing sales that Universal Nail had would have covered that. I tried to point that out to Ken, but his mind was made up. Somehow he thought that he could handle the overhead long enough for the cash to come rolling in, and he really liked the idea of keeping all the proceeds. That was a bit of a disappointment and ended my attempt to make collated nails. Other challenges occupied my time.

Needless to say, poor old Ken bought his $70,000 Wafio nail machine, and it was prominently reported in the *Fort Macleod Gazette*. He rented a workshop in Fort Macleod and, together with his girlfriend and Craig, set to work. Precisely what happened I don't really know, but a few months later he was insolvent. Wafios reclaimed its nail machine, and I purchased his unused wire and boxes for scrap value from the people liquidating the business. What a shame; it did not have to be that way. Fifty percent of a profit is so much better than 100 percent of nothing.

Interest rates were very high at that time, and I think we were paying about 13 percent on our revolving credit. Buying full truckloads of wire from Titan Steel resulted in us carrying too much debt, especially now that business had slowed down. Also, I had become suspicious that Titan was charging us for more wire than we were receiving. I asked Dan Kress if we could use his weigh scale when the truckload of wire arrived, and he said that would be all right. When Herb arrived, we weighed his truck, and after all the wire had been unloaded and the same number of empty wire carriers were on the truck (to replace the ones from the new delivery), we weighed it again, discovering that the load was a couple of hundred pounds or so light—not a lot, but enough to make me want to buy my wire elsewhere. I let Titan know that I was aware that I had been charged for more than they had shipped, and they were indifferent to my complaint.

Fortunately Stan Rutledge, who ran Davis Wire in Vancouver, was willing to sell us small loads at the price we were paying for twenty-ton loads, so I switched and bought from him. It made all the difference to be able to drive the Dodge up to Calgary with a load of nails for the office and customers and then go on to the Davis Wire depot on the east end of Calgary and pick up a seven-ton load of wire, which was the capacity of the truck. The manager in Calgary was Graham Frazer, who was always a pleasure to deal with. Buying smaller loads made a huge difference to our borrowing requirements, and the truck was loaded both ways, which saved on fuel—and it had a very thirsty motor. I figured out that at fifty-five miles per hour on the highway, it was consuming about a pint of petrol a minute. Even the most enthusiastic of beer drinkers would have had trouble keeping up with that for long.

I had known Stan for quite some time, as he had dropped in to see us when we first started. He had heard about what we were doing and had taken the trouble to visit us and check us out. He rather admired our courage to take on the big boys of the industry. To say that Stan was a good bloke would be a gross understatement. He went out of his way to help us, and his actions were about to totally transform Universal Nail.

(14)

———— ⚭ ————

MORRISON STEEL

THE PHONE RANG one day, and it was Stan advising me that Morrison Steel on Granville Island, Vancouver, had closed down, and he had heard that all the equipment was going to the scrap merchant. He suggested that I should drop everything, go straight there, and see what I could get. I took his advice, packed a bag, got in my car, and headed off to Vancouver.

Morrison Steel had been in business since the early years of the twentieth century, and as I entered the factory, it was evident that the place had been set up to run from a central power source, probably a steam engine, as there was an elaborate system of shafts and pulleys along the ceiling for belts to run all sorts of machines. In due course, the various machines had been fitted with electric motors, making the shafts and pulleys obsolete.

When I got there, everything was shut down except for the hot galvanizing equipment where they were processing the last of the nails that had come off the production line. The nails were thrown into these giant ovens together with chips of zinc. The gas burners then raised the temperature high enough to melt the zinc onto the nails as the ovens rotated. There were extractor fans and ducting to remove the highly toxic fumes from the room, but obviously the system was far from adequate because the room was filled with smoke.

There were machines all over the place, and the scrap merchant had a crew there that was unbolting them from the floor, lifting them up with an enormous forklift, driving them out to waiting trucks, and unceremoniously dropping them. As the machines were largely made of cast iron, this process was wrecking them as the castings would break. Fortunately I arrived early enough that they had not removed many of them, and the ones they were working on were antique National nail machines. Harry Irving had told me about National machines and advised me to stay away from them because they were primitive and would only make about eighty nails per minute. They were such interesting-looking antiques that I really wanted to buy one, as it should have been in a museum. It was such a shame that historic machines like that were being smashed. Regrettably, the scrapman wanted as much for those relatively useless machines as he wanted for the ones that were vitally important for my production line, so I could not justify buying one.

Right away I noticed that they had a Wafios S300, the biggest nail machine made. What an impressive piece of equipment! It weighed in at eight tons and was about sixteen feet long. I soon tracked down the scrap dealer and asked how much he wanted for the S300, and he told me that he had sold it about an hour before I got there, which was very disappointing.

I continued looking at the machinery, and it was all such a mess. Everything was so dirty and plastered in grease, it was difficult to tell which machines were in working order and which weren't. I decided to ask some of the people who were Morrison Steel workers and came across Hubert Bohm, who was exceedingly helpful.

I still get a Christmas card and letter each year from his wife, Theresa. Dear old Hubert is in an old folks' home; he is in his nineties and is rather frail. All those noisy machines made him as deaf as a post. It is amazing that the zinc smoke did not kill him long ago. Not only is he a good man, but he is also apparently as tough as nails too.

Getting back to the story, I explained to Hubert that I had a small nail factory and wanted to draw my own wire. I wanted to acquire a wire drawing machine, a nail tumbler, and packaging equipment as well. He took me on a tour of the place and showed me the good machines and told me which ones were worn out or had problems.

Most of the wire drawing machines had multiple reels, which would enable me to draw the wire down through multiple dies all in one process. Those machines were enormous and required staggering amounts of electrical power to run. Clearly, I could not afford those machines or even accommodate them with the amount of space they needed. Hubert had a suggestion and led me off to a single-reel bull block that had the ability to draw through one or two dies. It was a really old, dirty, and amazingly solid piece of equipment and was obviously made to last a very long time. It weighed about two tons, and after a brief discussion with the scrap dealer, I bought it for $1,200.

It was powered by a huge, direct-current, 220-volt, 70-horsepower electric motor that had a substantial control panel mounted on the wall next to it. That in turn was powered by a motor generator, which took the incoming 440-volt, three-phase power and converted it to 220-volt, single-phase direct current. The reason for the direct current motor was the incredible amount of torque (turning power) produced by such a motor. In the process of drawing wire, enormous turning power is required to start pulling wire through a die that reduces the diameter of that wire by a fraction of an inch. The energy required is so great that cold wire going into the die comes out the other side exceedingly hot. All that electrical equipment was really difficult to remove and load onto the truck. As it turned out, I did not need it, and it was all unnecessary. I will reveal more about that later.

Now I needed a flat-deck semi and right away. Stan located a truck and driver and sent him over to Granville Island. I continued with my shopping spree. This was incredible; I was able to buy equipment for just a few percent of what it would usually cost. I bought a Wafio S110 nail machine, a nail tumbler for polishing and coating the nails, and an overhead hoist. Then I was approached by a man who asked if I was interested in buying the Wafios S300.

As it turned out, this fellow had heard that I was on my way, and he knew what a valuable piece of equipment it was. He figured that I was bound to want it and purchased it for scrap value so he could flip it to me and make a few thousand for doing nothing. His thinking was correct. I imagine to the right purchaser it was probably worth $100,000. I imagine he paid somewhere between $2,000 and $4,000 for it, judging by the price I was paying the scrap dealer for the other machinery. He offered it to me for $15,000, which it was most definitely worth. I told him that $15,000 was way too much and asked him what he was planning to do with it. He said that he was going to move it to his plant and run it. I was convinced that he was lying and did not have anywhere to take it. He was relying on me to buy it. I offered him $4,000, and he said that was ridiculous.

I continued on my shopping spree. Not only did I have a limited amount of cash to spend, but I also had a twenty-ton limit on the weight allowance. I had to consider the amount of space available on the flat deck of the trailer. By now, it was late, and I left for the night.

The following day I continued looking around. The box packaging equipment was far too bulky and complicated for me to move; the same applied to the galvanizing machinery. Hubert came over to me and said that there was a small machine I really should buy as it worked well. He took me over to see the Humphrey fence staple machine, which I bought for $250. What a steal of a deal. That machine made perfectly good fence staples at six hundred per minute. A new fence staple machine would have cost about $30,000 and would have probably only been a little faster.

The man who was trying to sell me the Wafio S300 returned and tried again to get me to buy the machine, lowering his price to $10,000. I told him that I was not prepared to pay that and wished him well running it. He asked when I was leaving, and by then several machines had been loaded on my truck. I told him that by the end of the day, I would be finished and would not be coming back.

I continued with my purchases, picking up a small Glader Number 1 nail machine, a very small Wafios N series machine, and a few miscellaneous items like a weigh scale and an old railway-style, very heavy-duty push trolley. I still had hopes that I might yet be able to acquire the S300.

It was well into the afternoon, and the man returned yet again to try to make a deal. He admitted that he would really prefer me to buy it rather than go to all the trouble and expense of moving it, so he lowered his asking price to $8,000. I told him that I was preparing to leave, that my final offer was $5,000, and that I would not be coming back. He thought about it for a few minutes, came back, and accepted my offer. I paid him, and we loaded it on the truck with great difficulty, owing to its size and weight. The slightest mistake and vital parts would have been damaged. If that had happened, it would have added tens of thousands to my bill, as that machine was probably worth about $250,000 new, and parts would not have been cheap. A few days later, I found out that Wafios, the manufacturer, had sent a representative over to buy it, and they had arrived the next day. Apparently, they make very few of those big machines, and they wanted to buy it, renovate it, and resell it.

All the way home on my long drive I kept reflecting on what had just happened. I had spent about $8,000 buying machinery that would totally transform Universal Nail. The bull block was the most significant item. I would now be able to purchase coils of wire rod at about half the cost of finished wire and draw it myself. Stan had warned me that a lot of skill was required in the drawing process, and I might have difficulty mastering it. Setting the machine up and powering it was an enormous challenge, which I will come to later.

After writing this, I thought about Stan and how much he had helped me all those years ago. It made me think that I really should see if he was still alive so I could thank him for what he did. What were the chances? I calculated that if he was still around, he would be closer to ninety years old than eighty. It did not take long to find an old address book, and there I soon located not just the number for Davis Wire but also his home telephone number. I called it, and after several rings, it went to a generic recording. I proceeded to leave a message. I only got partway before being interrupted by the words, "Hello, Ed, you old bastard!" It was Stan. I recognized his voice, but I could tell that a lot of water had gone under the bridge since I had last heard it; it was not quite as booming as it used to be. I told him that I was writing the story of the Granum Gripper and had come to realize the enormous contribution he had made. I was phoning to thank him. We had a great conversation and talked for some time. He told me that he was now eighty-seven and still going to work each day. For the past few years he had been working at Lower Mainland Steel, and he had built it from a small concern into a thriving business with over five hundred employees and sold about twenty thousand tons a month of reinforcing bar. Good old Stan! It just shows, you can't hold a good man down, and you can take it to the bank that I am not the only one he has given a leg up to—a truly extraordinary man. Thank you, Stan.

(15)

———— ∞ ————

BUILDING PROJECT

I WASTED NO time getting home since I had to hire a crane service to unload all the heavy machinery. I also hired a steam-cleaning contractor so the machinery could be thoroughly cleaned before it was placed in the building. Getting everything off, cleaned, and stored away was a major undertaking. The building was nowhere near big enough to accommodate everything set up for production, so it had to be packed into every available empty space until the building could be extended.

Crane unloading Wafios S300 Nail Machine

Fortunately, at this stage, business had recovered from the impact of the National Energy Program, and the cash flow was good. Roy Hahn was now working for us full-time, and he was a highly intelligent young man. He learned what to do very quickly and was the best help

I ever had. I thoroughly enjoyed his sense of humour and companionship. He had a bit of a lazy streak in him at times, which actually turned out to be advantageous because he figured out better, more efficient ways of doing the job that saved on labour.

Recently, I managed to reach Roy on the telephone to let him know that I had included him in this book. It was the first time we had spoken in over thirty years. During our conversation, he told me of a memory he had from when he was sleeping over in our old bunkhouse. It was a warm summer

Roy Hahn

night, and his bed was close to the east-facing window. He was watching the distant flashing of purple lightning and enjoying the cool air coming in the window and the nearly complete silence when some words for a poem came into his head. He still remembered them all these years later.

We now had the machinery we needed to take us to the next level, but we could not get it set up and running because there simply was not enough room. Right away Jane and I looked at all the possibilities for expanding the building. After much deliberation, we decided to double the size of the building, and we gave the contract to Dandi Structures of Cardston. The company put up a well-insulated, wooden-framed building with steel cladding on the outside and drywall on the inside. It was eighteen feet high at the peak in the middle and twelve feet at the sides, and the floor was ten inches of highly reinforced concrete. The building was erected in very short order, and they did a superb job.

In went the electricity, and then we got to work on building an overhead hoist on the east side to lift the wire off the draw-ing machine and move it straight down to the far south end of the building. There, the wire could be  loaded onto reels lined up with the machines we were setting up along the west wall.

Not only were we incredibly busy setting up all the new equipment and reorganizing the entire factory, but business was increasing, and we needed more help in the factory. On one particular day, my help was unable to come in, and I was running everything. There were orders to be filled, and the pressure was on, so I really did not need too many distractions. Right on cue that distraction took place: A well-dressed visitor arrived and wanted to talk with me. It turned out that he was with Canada Manpower, a federal government agency, and he wanted to know if we needed more staff. I explained that his timing was perfect as my help had not showed up, and I really needed someone full-time. I proceeded to show him the requirements of the job. He left, advising me that he would bring a suitable candidate out the following day for a test run.

Sure enough, he returned with his "suitable candidate" the next day. He was a tall, thin black man from Somalia by the name of Ismail Mohammed Daoud, who was apparently an electrical engineer. He dropped him off and suggested that I try him out for the day, and he would pick him up later.

The first of the newly located nail machines was in place, and the conduit and wiring was also set up. All that remained to be done was to connect the wiring, and the machine would be ready to go. So see-ing that Ismail was an electrical engineer, I showed him the machine and asked him to wire it, explaining that the motor had been running on 440 volt, three phase, and as we only had 220 volt, three phase, he would need to reset the motor before connecting it.

I went back to running another machine and packing nails. Each time I looked across the room to see how he was getting on, he seemed to be doing nothing other than staring at the wires and scratching his head. After about ten minutes, I went over and asked him how he was getting on. The answer to that question was that he wasn't getting on at all. He was completely clueless, and the level of his electrical competence probably did not exceed the capability of changing a light bulb.

I wired in the motor and set Ismail to work packaging nails, which he managed to do all right.

When the man from Canada Manpower returned, I let him know that although Ismail was a likable fellow, he was singularly lacking in talent and was not worth anything close to what we paid our men. Right away he told me that they were prepared to reimburse us for most of his pay (I think it was about 80 percent) because he was a refugee. He also wanted to know if there was any way we could provide him with accommodation. I then made a very stupid and costly decision and agreed to hire Ismail.

As Jane and I had by that time replaced the broken windows in the old bunkhouse—the original dwelling on our property that was once the Jumbo Valley Post Office—we let Ismail stay there. He was rather a slow learner at the factory but became proficient at packaging nails and to a lesser extent running the machines. We liked Ismail, and he was good with our children. He particularly liked Robert, who was very young at that time.

Some time went by, and then the very definition of "a bad week" arrived, and I found out what a terrible decision I

Ismail with Robert

had made hiring him. Ismail only had a Somali driving license and needed to take a test to get an Alberta driving license. He asked if he could practice in our Datsun pickup, so I said that would be all right as long as he did not leave our property. We had ten acres, and the driveway was about a quarter of a mile long.

Obviously he did not understand what I had told him because he took off driving along the local gravel road. He went too fast, got into a slide, and rolled it in the ditch about two miles away. Ismail was somewhat battered and bruised and was feeling very sorry for himself, and our poor truck was totally destroyed. That was, without doubt, the best and toughest truck I have ever known, and he killed it. We towed the remains home and could not claim on the insurance as he did not have a valid license. It was a total loss.

Ismail's productivity in the factory was so lacking that he was barely worth the 20 percent of what we paid the other men, and after he destroyed the Datsun, I decided that he had to go. I phoned Canada Manpower and let them know that they could have him back. They asked me to go to their office in Lethbridge and fill in the necessary forms, and then they would take him back. I told Ismail to cycle into Granum to the factory the next morning and just package the nails that were already made because I did not trust him to run the machines unsupervised. Jane and I drove off to Lethbridge to fill out the forms. The drive went across open prairie where you can see for many miles. It was an exceedingly windy day, and we drove past some dried-up salt lakes where the wind was blowing up clouds of dust into the air.

On the way home, when we were about fifteen miles away, Jane spotted clouds of dust near our place, and we were trying to figure out where the dust was coming from. As we got closer, flashing lights became visible, and we came to the realization that something was on fire—and it had burned all the way to Ralph Poelman's place a quarter of a mile east of us. When we arrived home, we found the bunkhouse was ablaze. The Granum fire truck was there with a bunch of volunteers and a whole collection of neighbours enjoying the spectacle. It was quite a social gathering really, although it was very distressing for Jane and me. Apparently Ismail caused the fire when, being sufficiently stupid, he put ashes from the woodstove into a cardboard box and left the box on the wooden doorstep. He cycled off to work, and when the wind picked up, it set fire to the building. It seems poor old Ismail did not have a lot of intelligence to work with. It was a bit of a setback, but it was totally my fault.

There was one good thing that came as a result of that catastrophe, but we had to fight for it. Under our farm insurance policy, the outbuildings were covered for $20,000, so we put in a claim and an adjuster came out to appraise the situation. He told us that because the burned building was just one of several outbuildings, the $20,000 coverage would be spread amongst all of them, so they would only pay out $4,000 for the building, and the contents would be covered up to an additional $10,000. Ismail's belongings added up to about one hundred dollars, and that was it.

I thought about it for a while, and then had a brainwave: In the scullery of the brick house, there had been this most magnificent-looking, coal-burning cookstove. It looked wonderful but was essentially worthless because all the hotplates were broken, the cast-iron grate was burned out, and the walls had rust holes in them. I had moved it out to the bunkhouse and set it up in one of the rooms because it looked good, and I was planning to renovate it at some stage.

I called the insurance adjuster and listed all the contents that added up to less than a thousand dollars, and then I told him about the cookstove. He immediately told me that any stove connected to a chimney was considered part of the building and as such was not covered as contents. Right away, I pointed out that it was not connected to a chimney because I was working on restoring it. He said that if that was the case, it would be classified as contents, but from the pictures he had of the burned remains of the building, it looked to him like it was affixed to a chimney. Fortunately, I had a photograph of it sitting in the bunkhouse, and the picture clearly showed that it was not connected, so I sent him a copy of the picture.

On receiving the picture, he called me and confirmed that it was covered under the insurance and asked what I thought it was worth. I told him I had no idea and asked him to look into it and give me an idea what they thought it was worth. Personally, I think it was worth about fifty dollars.

A few days later he called and told me that it was worth between $1,900 and $2,100 and asked if we would be happy with $2,000. I said that would be just fine.

When we received the payment, we went to Calgary and purchased a brand-new Enterprise cookstove made in Sackville, New Brunswick. Amazingly enough, they were still making the same design of stove that they made back in 1910, and there were just a few slight improvements like enameling in the oven and the warming oven. Other than that, it looked precisely the same as the old ones, and the price was $1,800. I can't remember the name of the store, but I do remember the owner, Bob Wopenford, who was a most interesting man and knew a lot about wood and coal stoves.

We still have that stove in our kitchen, and I regularly cook my breakfast on it, especially if it is a cold morning. I suppose the lesson to be learned from our catastrophic encounter with Ismail is that quite often those dark storm clouds do indeed have a silver lining.

Having made nails for a few years, we had learned what was wrong with the way we were operating, so we set out to put things right. To make production more efficient, we constructed metal carts on big, heavy-duty casters with hooks welded on three sides and one end that would open. We made them so they held about five hundred pounds of nails and could be easily pushed around. We then welded stands on which to mount the nail machines that lifted them two and a half feet off the floor so the nail carts could be pushed into place under the production chutes. Alongside the machines welded to the stands were platforms to stand on so we would be the right height to work on the machines. The pressure was on to move quickly because during the reorganization, nail production was not possible, and I had to rely on Jane to do a lot of the deliveries so I could keep working on the fabricating and welding. We hired another very capable man at this time by the name of Gary Toews. He was reliable and hardworking, which was just what we needed at that critical stage.

Now the really challenging part of the job started. Somehow we had to get the wire drawing machine installed and running. We had three-phase, 220-volt power coming into the building, and there was a one-hundred-amp panel. I forget exactly how much power we needed for the bull block, but I know that it was 440 volt, and we did not have that. What I do remember clearly was that when I explained to Calgary Power what the machine needed, they quoted me $25,000 to upgrade the service and said there would be a maximum demand charge, which meant that if I ran that machine for just five minutes during the month, it would cost about $1,200. On top of that, we would have to pay the usual charge per kilowatt hour.

In the end, we could expect to pay as much as $2,000 per month for electricity if we were to connect the wire drawing machine. As it was, we were paying about $150 per month running the two nail machines and other equipment.

To pay that sort of money was out of the question, so we had to find a different way of powering it. I thought about it for a while and came to the conclusion that a diesel motor should be able to do the job, but that would cost a fortune to buy, so we would be no better off. Then I had a brainwave: what about using an old tractor motor? Well,

I had recently bought a 1955 McCormick Deering WD9 diesel tractor from Chick Calderwood, who had very generously sold it to me for one hundred dollars. It had a post pounder mounted on the front of it, which made the steering so heavy that it was extremely difficult to use, but the motor worked well. That was the answer, so we drove it to the nail factory and proceeded to pull it apart. On removing the motor and gearbox from the frame, it was plain to see that the shaft coming out of the back of the gearbox would not fit easily on to the shaft going into the wire drawing machine. Also, no matter which gear we used, the direction of rotation and the speed of rotation were wrong.

I figured out what we needed, took all the necessary measurements, and then got on the phone to machine shops in Lethbridge. I went to see a couple of them to get quotes on building a suitable gearbox and supplying a connecting shaft and universal joints. At a cost of $1,200 and a few weeks later, we mounted the extra gearbox and had everything bolted to the floor and connected. We ran the exhaust pipe straight up and through the ceiling and were ready for testing. I knew that the electric motor we had taken off was 70 horsepower and the replacement tractor motor was approximately 50 horsepower, so it was likely to be a bit underpowered, but I also thought that the big, old diesel motor was not short of torque, and that was what we needed. We connected a long 1½-inch pipe to the original clutch pedal to give good leverage. On firing up the motor and testing all the gears, everything worked perfectly.

By this time a load of wire rod coils had been delivered. They weighed around a ton each, and we had fabricated a giant carrier for the rod and a giant reel dispenser so we could rotate the rod coils, allowing the rod to feed into the machine. We placed the dispenser forty feet away so, in the event of it jamming, there would be about ten seconds for us to disengage the motor before the reel crashed into the wire drawing machine. This turned out to be a good plan as the rod did indeed jam on a fairly regular basis, and the sound of the reel being dragged across the floor was very noticeable, but we always managed to

BUILDING PROJECT 93

shut the machine down before impact. Ten seconds does not sound like much time, but when working in the factory we had to be exceedingly alert especially when several machines were running at the same time.

It was common for one person to be drawing wire, running two nail machines and the nail tumbler, and boxing up nails at the same time. One had to be very alert to all the different sounds, and the noise in there was intense. Even with ear protection, it was noisy. Every machine had distinctive sounds, and if there was a problem, the sound would often change. The reels feeding wire into the nail machines sometimes jammed and would be dragged across the floor. You had to be very quick to shut them off, as there were only about six seconds before the reel would impact the wire straightener, and then the wire would snap. That was not a huge problem as it only took a few minutes to move the reel back and reconnect the wire, but in the case of the wire drawing machine, it would take about fifteen minutes and a lot of work to restart production.

We fitted the dies in the wire drawing machine and tested it.

I have just described the process involved, and my description filled a whole page. On reading it through, I realized that only engineering enthusiasts would be interested in that, and everyone else would close the book and read no further, so here is the short version:

We fed the wire rod into the wire drawing machine through the descaler and flux applicator and die, three times around the skirt of the reel, around the idler wheel, into the second flux box, and into the second die onto the top part of the reel.

The moment of truth had arrived. Would it work? We engaged first gear, with the motor running gently, and let out the clutch. The capstan reel turned slowly, and everything appeared to be working just fine, but production would be rather slow at that pace. We stopped it, changed to fourth gear, gave it about half throttle, and let out the clutch. The motor groaned a bit as it picked up speed, but soon it was running perfectly. We increased the throttle up to full working power, and it performed brilliantly. What a relief!

Edward drawing wire.

Drawing 5.5mm wire rod down to six gauge on the first die and then down to eight gauge on the second die made wire at the rate of about 650 pounds per hour. Eight-gauge wire was the right diameter for four-inch nails. If we needed to make 3¼-inch nails, the wire had to be drawn again through one die to bring the diameter down to ten gauge or two dies for eleven and twelve gauge.

Having that machine reduced our costs immensely, and the diesel motor was so cheap to run; it was amazing. The monthly cost of diesel was about $160, which compared very favourably with Calgary Power's projected cost of around $2,000 per month after the one-time upgrade cost of $25,000.

The McCormick Deering diesel motor.

(16)

New Machinery

THE MOST IMPORTANT new machine was now running, and as a result our input cost of the wire was substantially reduced. We also had the distinct advantage of being able to draw any diameter of wire we wanted even if it was not within the tolerance of a recognized gauge.

When you take into consideration that the strength of a piece of wire increases considerably as it gets thicker, it was not necessary to increase the diameter of the shaft of a nail very much to increase its resistance to bending enormously. As one of the great concerns of our customers was the nails' resistance to bending, we made the shafts of our nails a few thousandths of an inch broader than our competition. By doing that we were legitimately able to claim what we had written prominently on our boxes: "Granum Grippers, the Tough Ones."

John Dinsdale drawing wire.

They were tougher than all the others, and most people thought that we were using a better grade of steel, but it was just that our nails were simply that little bit thicker. There were just a few less nails in a pound, but looking at the nail, the difference was difficult to spot.

Another significant piece of equipment added to our production line was the nail tumbler. This was a very substantial horizontal drum that would hold around a thousand pounds of nails. The process involved putting the nails into the drum with about enough sawdust to fill a two-gallon bucket, securing the lid and running the machine for about an hour. The drum would rotate about fifty times a minute; the nails would tumble around inside the drum, and the action of them crashing into each other and hitting the outside of the drum took the sharp edges off the points of the nails and polished them. The sawdust absorbed the oil, grease, and dirt, and over the course of the hour, the sawdust—together with the small chips of steel produced by the action of cutting the points—would be thrown out onto the floor through a screen and the small gap around the lid.

With the introduction of the nail tumbler, we were able to improve our nail coating system. Rather than phosphate-coat the nails in a hot acid tank, we used a paint-like chemical called Syncoat 3304. After the nails had been tumbled for an hour and polished clean, we added about a gallon of this chemical and ran the machine for about two minutes, emptied it into a big tray, and then dumped the nails onto the packing table ready to be boxed using the electromagnetic nail aligner. For the first few minutes, the fumes coming off the nails while they dried were somewhat acrid, so lots of ventilation was required. We could get Syncoat in any colour we liked, so we made our nails royal blue; they looked distinctive and appealing. When the nails were driven into the wood, the plastic-like coating was heated by the friction and tended to act like glue, making the nail resistant to being removed.

Southern Alberta is a very windy place, and there are numerous occasions when trucks get blown over and roofs are torn off buildings, and it has even caused houses to get blown off their foundations. As the area tends to be semiarid, the combination of dry conditions and wind can be deadly when a fire breaks out. The reason I mention this is to lay the foundation for an incident that took place one windy afternoon in Granum.

Gary and I were making nails, and the big doors were open wide as usual. It was warm and dry, and the wind was blowing at about forty miles per hour, which was causing the doors to bang and crash a bit. After securing them as best I could, I commented to Gary that it would be a terrible day for a fire. A short while later we heard the fire alarm go off at the Granum Fire Hall. We shut down the machines and watched to see where the fire truck was heading. Before the truck even started, we noticed a small amount of smoke coming from the Alberta Hotel. We walked over the railway tracks to the hotel and could see a bit of smoke coming out of an upstairs window that appeared to be partially open.

The fire crew turned up a few minutes later and proceeded to connect the hoses to hydrants in preparation to fight the fire. This process seemed to take quite a long time, and as they started to spray water on the building, the fire had grown to a serious conflagration. Windows started to break with the heat of the fire, which allowed the wind to fan the flames, and the fire positively exploded. Thick smoke, burning debris, and showers of sparks were blowing to the northeast directly toward the post office, the other side of the road, and across the railway tracks for about two hundred yards to the Alberta Wheat Pool elevator.

The fire crew was spraying water on the Alberta Hotel, which was a lost cause, but they had the good sense to soak down the post office and save the building. It was obvious to me that the elevator, although a long way off, was in danger because not only was it a very large and dry wooden structure, but there also was a lot of dry grass around the base of the building, which could so easily catch fire if the burning sparks got that far. I alerted the fire chief to the danger and suggested that some of his men go over to the elevator and hose down the base of the building and the grass. I said that Gary and I could help if necessary. He was obviously irritated by my suggestion and told me to mind my own business; he knew what he was doing.

Over the next fifteen minutes or so, the blaze was so intense that the hotel came crashing down, and the gale force wind blew not only sparks but sizable pieces of burning material right at the elevator into the dry grass, which caught fire and in turn ignited the building. It simply took off, and within a few minutes that too was a towering inferno that made the Alberta Hotel fire look small.

Of course, the Granum fire was widely reported on television and radio and in the newspapers, and as a result, I soon received a phone call.

The caller asked, "Aren't I giving you enough business? Was it really necessary to burn down our elevator?" It was John Bilan, who could not help notice the irony of buying Granum Grippers and having the Granum elevator burn to the ground. It amused him to tease me about it.

Setting up the Wafios S300 was quite a challenge due to its immense size and weight. We moved it very slowly across the floor, pushing it with the forklift. We had jacked it up, placed substantial timbers under the legs, and placed two-inch in diameter tubes under the timbers so we could roll it to the far end of the building. When we got it there, we welded one-foot-high stands, jacked up the machine, bolted the stands onto the legs, and lowered it to the ground. We then drilled bolts into the floor to anchor it in place.

Norm Oliver down in Pennsylvania had made dies in three gauges and several sets of cutters for the machine, which we fitted. Then we set it up, ready for testing. The setup

Gary Toews and the Wafios S300.

was exactly the same as for the Wafio S110; it was just much bigger. We made six-inch, eight-inch, ten-inch, and twelve-inch nails on that machine, and it made them at the rate of two a second. For twelve-inch nails, it took about seventy seconds or so to make enough nails to fill a fifty-pound box.

Interestingly enough, everyone was rather nervous about running that machine, and most of the time it was going, I was running it. The thump of the header die forging the head of each nail was so great that if you sat on the concrete a hundred feet away, you could just about feel it. The finished nails came down the production chute at great speed, and it was a bit hazardous checking the nails, which had to be done very often to make sure that the machine was not going out of adjustment. Hundreds of pounds of useless junk could easily be made if you were not paying attention. On one occasion a twelve-inch nail came down the chute and hit my wrist point first. It cut right through my clothing and opened up the flesh on my wrist badly enough to require a few stitches to put me back together again.

Needless to say, I could not find enough business to run that machine very often. My best customer for the big nails was Davis Walker in Kent, Washington. Yes, you guessed it. Good old Stan Rutledge got me the business. Davis Wire in Canada was associated with Davis Walker in Kent, Washington, and Stan introduced me to the plant manager, Pete Cronin. Davis Walker made huge quantities of nails, but the company did not have the necessary machinery to make any nails longer than five inches. We agreed on prices and made all of its bigger sizes, packaging them in Davis Walker boxes.

I thought that we should let the end users know where the nails were made, so inside each box was a nicely printed sheet of paper that said the nails were made with great care by Universal Nail of Granum, Alberta, population 325. The message ended with us thanking them for buying our nails. It did not take long before Pete was on the phone, rather irritated that we were putting those pieces of paper in the boxes without consulting him first. I pointed out that we took great pride in making good-quality nails and would not want people to know that we made them if they were junk.

The Wafios S110 was mounted next to the original S110, and beside the Glader Number 2, we set up the Humphrey fence staple machine. The remaining Glader Number 1 and the small Wafio N series machine were never set up and just collected dust in the corner of the building.

Some months after getting everything going, we had a big drive to clean up the place and make it look more cheerful. Everything was thoroughly cleaned up and painted yellow and blue. The men treated the machines with more respect when they were clean and looked good. At that point, John Dinsdale had joined the team.

Machines from the left: Wafios S300, Wafios S110, Wafios S110, Glader Number 2 and Humphrey.

To enter the factory and see everything looking clean and tidy was very satisfying, and I was proud to show visitors around. In fact, we had a steady stream of visitors, and thinking back to those days compared with today, I cannot imagine any factory allowing visitors into such a potentially dangerous place. Everywhere you looked there was machinery clattering away that could tear off limbs or hurl projectiles in your direction, but no visitor ever got hurt, and we must have had a lot over the years. In fact, thinking about many tourist attractions that are open to the public today, most of them are downright boring compared to the nail factory tour.

One attraction that immediately comes to mind is the Head-Smashed-In Buffalo Jump west of Fort Macleod. It is situated on Jamie Calderwood's land, and Jane and I went to have a look at it years before the Alberta provincial government spent millions of dollars building a museum that looks like a concrete gun emplacement. We went to the place to check it out, and for a fee we could walk around the building and see a bunch of stuffed buffalos in the process of jumping off a small cliff. In addition there was a collection of sheets of painted plywood with pictures and text describing how the buffalo were panicked into stampeding over the cliff. There was also a short, poorly produced film. Thousands of people go there, but there really is not much to see. Maybe they have improved it since we went; I sincerely hope so because it was a bit of a yawn.

Before they built the gun emplacement, you could see all the fragments of buffalo bone on the ground at the foot of the cliff and imagine what it would have been like when it was in use. Very few people went there at that time, but I think it was much better then.

Our ability to draw our own wire totally transformed the business by greatly improving our profit margin. The diesel motor worked exceedingly well running the wire drawing machine, but it did sweat rather a lot of oil onto the floor. To stop the oil from spreading everywhere, we threw wood shavings down to absorb it. The leak was not bad enough for us to stop production and replace gaskets on the motor, so we just ignored it.

After a few months of production, a crack developed where the rail supporting the overhead hoist was welded to the cross member above the diesel motor. I asked Gary if he would spend a few minutes and reweld the crack. I drove the forklift over with a pallet for Gary to stand on, passed him the wires from the arc welder and a few rods, and hoisted him up high enough to work on the rail. I switched on the welder and went back to packaging nails.

A few minutes later I heard Gary calling me in a rather distressed state. I looked over to where he was, and I could not see him for the smoke. Sparks falling from twelve feet in the air where he was welding had fallen onto the oil-soaked wood shavings, and they had caught fire. The fire was burning vigorously, and the thick black smoke had completely engulfed Gary. I shouted out to him to stay where he was, and I would sort out the problem. I grabbed a fire extinguisher, rushed over to the fire, and managed to put it out in about six seconds. Those dry-powder fire extinguishers are incredible and amazingly effective. In a minute or two, the smoke had dissipated enough to be able to see Gary again, and he was greatly relieved to be lowered to the ground.

Moral of the story: It's probably not a good idea to allow a pile of oil-soaked wood shavings to build up right below where you are going to do a spot of arc welding. Secondly, if a fire breaks out, don't panic; take a fire extinguisher, aim the jet of powder at the base of the fire, and sweep from side to side across the fire for the length of the blaze until it is out.

You will remember me telling the story of Greg Tetz, the forklift operator at the Alberta Wheat Pool who managed to get a job in the purchasing department. Well, as it turned out, giving him a leg up by encouraging John Bilan to bring him into his purchasing department ended up saving me from an absolute catastrophe. You see, just as things were really starting to go well, John Bilan had a massive heart attack and died at the age of fifty-three. What a shock that was! Not only was he a very fine fellow and a huge supporter of Universal Nail, but because of his incredible generosity, we were selling our nails to the Wheat Pool for about nine dollars a box more than they could get them from Macmillan Bloedel. Admittedly, about four dollars of that could be justified by there being more nails per pound, but it would have been difficult to explain away the other five dollars.

As soon as I heard the bad news, I asked who would be taking over his job as purchaser. His secretary was not sure but had heard that the likely candidate was going to be some outsider. I scheduled an appointment to see the new purchaser as soon as he started. A couple of weeks had gone by, and I went to meet the new purchaser. I arrived in the office, and the receptionist advised me that he was busy but would be available in a few minutes. I was working up a bit of a sweat trying to figure out how I was going to justify charging so much when she told me that I could go down the hallway to his office. As I walked in the door, I could hardly believe my good fortune, as Greg welcomed me and assured me that John had fully briefed him on everything, and it would be business as usual.

Even though we no longer lived in Granum, we nearly always attended social events at the Blunden Hall for occasions like the New Year's dance. These were always well attended, and they were a great opportunity to socialise with everyone. You will remember me relating stories about Clarence De Maere. Well, Clarence had a brother named Albert, and Albert was also a very nice fellow, but he was a bit "wobbly." He obviously had a soft spot for Jane because at every dance, he would head straight over to her at the earliest opportunity and request a dance. Jane said that he was always charming, but she was terrified that he might drop dead at any moment as he was so frail and unsure on his feet. Needless to say, that never happened.

Sometimes the music was good, and on other occasions it was not so good. On one memorable occasion, there was an old couple—one playing the piano and the other a fiddle. To say that the music was bad would be a gross understatement. It was so excruciatingly terrible that it drove everyone to drink. The dance floor was empty, and everyone hit the bottle. The vast majority of those attending that night became totally paralytic. I have never seen anything like it before or since.

(17)

─── ∽∾ ───

ECONOMY OF SCALE

AT LAST, WE had everything we needed to really rock and roll. With the ability to get our biggest input cost down substantially by drawing our own wire, we could make a good profit on our regular sales, and we could compete at the wholesale level and still clear a profit.

Our customer base was now sufficiently large, and the profit margin was high enough that we were doing all right, but we had the capacity to make a lot more product than we were selling. Bearing in mind the fact that the fixed overhead cost per box became less with each additional box made per day, the focus was on increasing sales so we could get that production up and keep it up. Thanks again to Stan Rutledge; he introduced me to Bill Hammer of Marathon Forest Products in Edmonton, which manufactured oriented strand boards (OSB) and was a wholesaler of dimensional lumber. That was right at the time when OSB was rapidly replacing sheets of plywood owing to the lower cost.

I talked with Bill about the possibility of him distributing our nails in the Edmonton area and explained that we were selling directly to building contractors from Red Deer south, but from Edmonton and to the north, we had very few customers. I also explained that it was necessary to manufacture more than a certain number of boxes per day in order to keep the fixed overhead cost per box down to an acceptable level. What I proposed was for Bill to buy our surplus stock at a little over what it cost us to make it when we accumulated too much. He agreed, and the plan worked very well. It seemed so appropriate that we were selling nails to Mr. Hammer.

Bill was not greedy, and as he was buying the nails at a good price, he sold them to his customers at a very competitive price. I would phone him whenever I had too much stock, and he would place an order for seven tons, which was the capacity of the Dodge, and I would then deliver.

Sometimes his sales were so good that he was placing orders before I had even built up a surplus, so we had to work a bit harder and longer.

Around that time, I had converted the heating system in the old brick house back to coal. It had been fitted with natural gas burners so I removed them and upgraded the chimney. It was a massive cast-iron boiler that circulated hot water to cast-iron radiators throughout the

NAILED IT

house by convection through two-inch-diameter pipes. It worked incredibly well and was very economical to run on coal. As there were no active coal mines near Granum, I bought it at Wabamun, thirty miles west of Edmonton. I would deliver my load of nails to Bill Hammer, which was about a five-hour drive and then spend the night at a motel. The next morning I would head out to Wabamun and pick up a load of coal at sixteen dollars a ton and drive home to Granum. One full seven-ton load would last for most of the winter.

On one trip home with a load of coal, I experienced more excitement than I had bargained for. As I was approaching a red traffic light at the intersection of Whitemud and Calgary Trail at the south end of Edmonton, I put my foot on the brake, and the pedal went all the way to the floor with little resistance; I had close to total brake failure. With seven tons of coal on board, the truck was in no hurry to stop. I changed down through the gears as fast as I could and applied the parking brake, but there was no way that I was going to be able to pull up in time, so I blasted the horn and barged my way into the traffic as I turned hard right. Fortunately everyone managed to swerve around me. It was a somewhat nerve-racking experience.

A short distance down the road was a shopping mall where there was an automotive parts outlet. I pulled in there and checked to see what had happened. The brake fluid reservoir was empty, so I bought a big container of the stuff and filled up the reservoir. Being on my own, I could not bleed the air out of the system properly, but I soon discovered what the problem was. There was damage to the brake line near one of the front wheels, and every time that I had applied the brakes, fluid had been leaking out. I had noticed that the brakes were getting a bit spongy, but of course the point had been reached where the fluid completely ran out and there were no brakes. After I filled up with fluid, the brakes worked fairly well, but the fluid was squirting out of the hole quickly, so I would only be able to use the brakes a few times before they would fail again. I took great care and managed to drive all the way home without using the brakes at all.

On my trips to Edmonton, I called on other potential customers and managed to get another good one. Ernie Desroches ran Nu-Hawk Distributors, which was rather like Hillhurst Hardware in Calgary. The company targeted building contractors, and Ernie was prepared to sell nails with just a small markup. His customers loved the Granum Gripper, and soon he was buying large quantities. It worked out very well because I could deliver to Marathon and Nu-Hawk at the same time, and I could split the load so they did not have to buy a full seven tons each time.

As you can imagine, the wear and tear on the vehicles was considerable, and I needed the services of a good mechanic to keep everything running.

Mel Mensinger outside the Standard Garage.

Fortunately, right on the main street of Granum, Mel Mensinger ran the Standard Garage, and he did all maintenance and repairs. He was a great character and loved to knock back quite a few drinks on a regular basis. He was obviously very skilled because he always turned out good work even when he was somewhat inebriated.

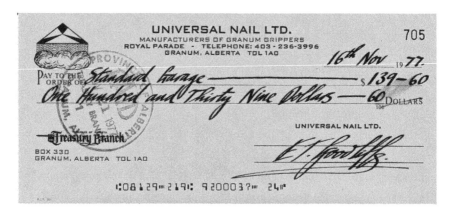

John Dale gave me notice that he no longer wanted to share the Calgary office. At that point we could have afforded to rent the whole place on our own, but it had worked out so well sharing with people who could cover for me when I was not there, I rather wanted things to continue that way. I advertised in the paper and ended up sub-renting to Bill Raynard, who together with his father, Earl, ran Raynard Automotive, which supplied tyre shops with supplies like patches, rubber solution, valve stems, lead weights, etc. This time around, I managed to sub-rent for the total amount that I was paying, which was really handy. Bill and Earl were good people, and we got on very well. They covered for me so well when I was not there, it would have been tough to get any better service from employees on our payroll. It struck me as amusing that a business supplying tyre repair supplies should be sharing a building with a nail manufacturer. Anyone would think that I must be dropping nails all over the place to improve their business.

(18)

ENCOURAGING SMALL BUSINESS

As TIME WENT by, I became more and more aware of the gross hypocrisy of what the politicians kept telling us. Every time there was an election at any level of government, every candidate would go on about how much they supported small business and how their proposed policies were designed to help and encourage that sector of the economy. Nothing could have been further from the truth. From my personal experience running Universal Nail, it was glaringly obvious that they were very concerned about looking after the big multinational corporations and totally indifferent to the plight of businesses such as Universal Nail. We were not operating in a free market economy; it more closely resembled what Benito Mussolini referred to as corporatism or corporate fascism, where the big corporations and the state work closely together for their mutual benefit. Taxes and regulations were designed to hobble the small businesses and reduce the competition for the big boys, who could then maximize their profits.

There were two glaring examples of where they demonstrated their indifference to small business that directly affected Universal Nail:

As manufacturers, we were required to collect a 7 percent federal sales tax on the nails we made. The tax authorities told us that we had to base that 7 percent tax on our selling price and remit the cash to them monthly, and there were large penalties for late payments.

At one point, I purchased some wire from a major Canadian manufacturer of nails. I was talking with its representative about the federal sales tax. Being a manufacturer, we were exempt from paying the tax on the purchase of the wire, but we had to charge it on our finished product, which was a lot more valuable than the wire, and I told him that it took a big chunk out of our profit. The tax was hidden so our customers had no idea that around $1.70 a box was going to the federal government. He suggested that we were doing it all wrong. He thought the big manufacturers did not have to collect 7 percent of their selling price; they had an "agreed price" that they had negotiated with the Canadian Tax Authorities regardless of the size or type of nail. He thought that price was ten dollars per box or 65.4 cents a box in tax, less than half of what we were paying. For our nails, which we sold at between twenty-four and thirty dollars per box, the tax was $1.57 per box in tax for the cheaper ones and $1.96 for the higher-priced ones.

Apparently the government of Canada was so concerned about small business that they forced us to charge between 240 percent and 300 percent more tax on our product than the big boys had to pay. It does not take much brainpower to figure out that the increased price we had to charge made us less competitive, and so our sales would be reduced accordingly.

I contacted Revenue Canada and requested to be treated the same as Stelco, and I was informed that the reduced rate only applied to the big manufacturers. Next, I went to my member of Parliament who found out the same information. He then queried the minister of finance, who asked how many voters there were at Universal Nail, and my MP replied that there were four. The finance minister let him know that for four votes, he was indifferent to our plight. It is such a shame that the general public has no idea how little the politicians really care about small business.

The second major impediment was the freight subsidy that the government of Canada offered to Ontario and Quebec manufacturers. I found out about it when I had an enquiry from a prospective Ontario customer. I discovered that it would cost us four dollars per box freight to ship our nails to Ontario, and yet I had found out that manufacturers in Ontario and Quebec were shipping to Calgary and Edmonton for one dollar per box. Apparently, the government of Canada was subsidising it to the tune of three dollars per box. It was something to do with the "crow rate," and I think the original stated intent was to give the central Canadian manufacturers a competitive advantage over competitors from the United States, but it has also done a great job of destroying the manufacturing base of Western Canada.

Not many months were to pass by before I discovered another massive tax that was about to be levied on Universal Nail. There had been a municipal election in Granum; Ege Mohr had retired with several other councillors. There was a new mayor and some new councillors. They were spending a lot and were in desperate need of additional funds like so many other town councils.

Granum, being a small town with very few commercial enterprises, did not have much of a tax base, so they were without doubt in a difficult position. I don't know who made the discovery, but someone had been studying the provincial legislation on the taxing powers of local authorities, and that resulted in a provincial government property tax assessor visiting me at the nail factory. He told me that he was there to reassess my factory for tax purposes and proceeded to ask me all sorts of questions about the machinery in the building. That seemed very odd, so I asked him what relevance that had to the valuation on the building and land. He went on to explain that under the municipal act, not only were the building and land taxable, but all of the industrial machinery was also taxable, and I had a lot of machines. I pointed out that the machines were very old and not worth much. He countered by telling me that they made their assessment according to replacement value of new equipment less a small percentage for depreciation.

When he had finished, I asked what difference it was going to have on the amount of tax we would have to pay, and it was going to be devastating. The municipal tax was going to take the lion's share of everything we were making. The only piece of good news was that it would take at least a year before it was implemented.

I went straight to the town office to find out when the next council meeting was scheduled and asked to have the opportunity to speak to the council. I went to the meeting and told them what I had learned from the tax assessor. I let them know that I had been most appreciative of Ege Mohr and the council back in 1975 giving me the land, but I pointed out the many thousands that had since been paid in property taxes that would never have been received by the town if Ege had not been so far-sighted. On top of that, I pointed out that because of the economic activity generated by Universal Nail, people had been employed and money had been spent in the town raising the living standard for everyone. At that time Universal Nail was one of the biggest taxpayers in town, and the tax was about to increase dramatically. I told them that the huge increase in tax was likely to kill the goose laying the golden eggs. Why would I work for almost nothing? They did not seem to be too concerned with my plight; in fact I got the impression that some of them were quite enjoying having me cornered. They explained that it cost a lot to run the Town of Granum, and "we all have to pay our share." They needed the money, and the municipal act allowed them to assess my machinery, so I did not really have any choice other than to pay. They said it was out of the question for us to negotiate a lower amount that we could afford to pay.

That hit me like a ton of bricks; it felt to me that we were fully paying our share, and it was beyond unreasonable for us to have to pay more. I had done everything I could to make our nails as competitive as possible and make the best nail that money could buy, and here they were setting themselves up to steal most of the wealth we were generating. Looking back on it, I can see that it was typical socialism in action.

Their philosophy is all about "sharing the wealth," which means taking from those who are generating it and giving it to those who are not. Invariably for every one generating wealth, there are always a lot more who are not or who are only generating minimal wealth. As a result, it often ends up that the enterprising ones who drive the economy get punished with high taxes, and they respond by ceasing to produce wealth, but the unproductive members of society still have to be paid, which leads to mounting public debt and eventual economic collapse.

Jane and I talked it over and realized that we needed to step back, consider all the options, and make a decision on what to do next. I visited Ege Mohr to see what advice he might offer. Ege was a wise man and a sound thinker, and he listened carefully to what I had to say, and he was about as shocked as I was. After I had explained our financial predicament, and he could see the huge percentage of our earnings that were going to be claimed by the Town of Granum, he said that he would fully understand if we decided to shut down the business.

It was such a ridiculous situation. We had never been in such good shape: we had plenty of regular customers, we had reduced our input costs, we were making a first-class product, we had earned a good reputation in the marketplace, and we had reliable employees. Why would we walk away from that?

We thought long and hard about it and considered how the municipal tax was effectively going to take my income. Could I increase the profit enough to cover what they were going to take? Not too likely with increased competition from China looming, the ever-increasing erosion of the traditional nail market from collated nails for pneumatic guns, and of course the government subsidy of my central Canadian competitors and the extra sales tax the federal government was taking from me.

One more thing that was enough to make my blood boil was foreign-owned Tree Island Steel located in Richmond, British Columbia, went broke, and the federal government rescued it with a multimillion-dollar bailout.

So to recap the situation: The federal government was subsidising my competitors from the east and bailing out my competitors in the west. On top of that they were singling us out to pay considerably more federal sales tax on our product compared with anyone else, and the town council was about to deal the death blow by doubling our town taxes. So much for encouraging small business. Actions speak louder than words, and we were getting the message loud and clear.

Would selling the business be an option? The simple answer to that was no. The taxes were about to make it uneconomical for us, so it would be just as uneconomical for anyone else. Anyway, at that time you could get about 10 percent on your money by simply putting it in a deposit account at the bank. Our business was making about 10 percent net on turnover, so why would you do all that work when you could just stick your money in the bank and do nothing?

We figured out that the best strategy was to effectively drive the business at full speed over the cliff into extinction. If we announced to the world that we were shutting down, we would have had a lot of customers simply not paying their bills, which would have been a disaster, and all our stock on hand would be sold at fire-sale prices. With that thought in mind, we decided that we were going to take a year to shut the business down. We were going to keep that secret from all but our best regular customers. We were going to let them know so they could be fully stocked when we finally closed the doors. The plan was to stop manufacturing the slow-moving sizes and types of nails and keep manufacturing the fast movers so everything would run out at the same time, and we could maximize the price we received for our nails. During the first few months, it was very much business as usual, and then bit by bit, the pace picked up. Virtually all of our longtime regular customers had grown to like our nails, and they placed huge orders so they would have lots on hand when we closed down. The last few months were the best and most profitable we'd ever had, which made it all the more emotionally devastating to just shut it all down.

It was in February 1985 that the machines finally went silent. I was on my own in the factory. I ran off the last coil of wire rod, and the old diesel was running smoothly as it always did. It ran faultlessly for hundreds of hours and never let us down. Chick Calderwood's one-hundred-dollar tractor had done us proud. On the last day, only the Glader was running, and it was making 3¼-inch nails. All was quiet as I packaged up the last boxes. All these years later, I still have a few of those nails left as I saved more than a ton of Granum Grippers for my own use.

There was nobody but me to witness the death of the Granum Gripper; ten years had gone by since we started. Unlike the crowds that witnessed the first nails being produced, there was nobody but me to witness the last gasp. What an adventure it had been, and what a heartbreaking moment that was.

Word had spread that we were closing down, and a local auctioneer approached me and offered to buy everything for a very small amount. I seem to remember it was about $12,000, and there was absolutely no way I was going to accept that.

Faced with the harsh reality of Universal Nail closing down, Jane and I felt that it would be too depressing to stay in the Granum area and decided that we should move and start afresh somewhere else. So much effort had gone into the business, and we had an enormous emotional attachment to it, as well as the old brick house that we had totally trans-formed. What happy days we had in that magnificent house. Also the town of Granum felt like home. We arrived as total strangers but had put down deep roots. Our whole reason for being there was crashing and burning; we simply had to leave and close that chapter of our lives.

There had been several years of drought at Granum and a plague of grasshoppers, and the seemingly endless wind was something we would not be sorry to leave. Having made lots of trips to Edmonton deliver-ing nails, I had thought that the countryside around the city was most agreeable. I particularly liked the fact that there were lots of trees. We decided to look for somewhere to live within about sixty or so miles from Edmonton.

(19)

———⚬⚬⚬———

A New Beginning

By the summer of 1984 we were planning to put our house up for sale. We had purchased the place for $30,000 and had spent about another $30,000 renovating it. Countless hours of work had also gone into the project, and as far as we were concerned, it was a truly outstanding and unique old house. It was in perfect condition and was situated on ten acres of land, so we thought it had to be worth quite a lot.

We went to the real estate agent in Claresholm and discussed the possibility of listing our property. They wanted 7 percent commission, and they valued the house at $60,000. They warned us that as it was rather a big house, it might be difficult to sell and could take a long time. We were shocked that their valuation was so low. Five years had gone by since we bought the place, and inflation had driven up house prices by a significant amount during that time, so how could it be so worthless? We went and talked with another agent in Lethbridge who also valued it at $60,000.

Reflecting on the situation, it appeared that we had spent all that effort and money and would not even get our capital back in dollar terms, let alone keep up with inflation. That was simply not good enough; we decided that if the agents were too pathetic to be able to sell our property for a reasonable amount, we would have to do the job ourselves and save the 7 percent commission.

In the autumn we took the plunge and placed adverts in the Lethbridge, Fort Macleod, and Claresholm papers. Beneath the picture, the wording offered, "this magnificent 1917 vintage, fully restored, three-storey brick house with solid oak doors, wooden paneling, etc. on 10 acres of land for $103,000."

The response was immediate, and the phone was red hot with people expressing interest. Over the following couple of weeks, we showed the house to about forty prospective purchasers. We sold it, and we got the full $103,000. It was rather satisfying to get $43,000 more than the real estate agents said it was worth and keep the $4,000 and change in commission. The newspaper adverts were about $500, and they worked incredibly well.

With our home sold and the new owner due to take possession in December, the pressure was on to find a new home. We headed to Edmonton, checked into a hotel, and set to the job at hand. We managed to get hold of a multiple listing book after visiting a few agents, which made the job a lot easier. Initially, we set a limit of $200,000 and looked for properties about forty to sixty miles out of Edmonton. Ideally, we wanted the house to be on a quarter section (160 acres) of land and have plenty of trees on the property.

It turned out that there were very few properties that were even remotely suitable, and we made the rash decision to raise our limit to $350,000, even though we really could not afford that much, justifying it by assuming it would be possible to negotiate the price down a bit. What a good decision that turned out to be. We found a listing for a big house comprising four thousand square feet of developed space on the ground and first floor, with another three thousand square feet of an undeveloped walk-out basement. On top of that, it had six hundred square feet of undeveloped "granny annex" above the two-car attached garage. It also had a substantial Quonset, and it was on a quarter section (a quarter of a square mile) with about one hundred acres of trees. The listed price was $325,000.

Linda, the real estate agent, took us out to view the property on a rainy day. The house was a couple of miles down a very muddy road, and she had a great deal of difficulty staying out of the ditch. The owner greeted us at the door and invited us in. He told us his name was Eder, but his friends called him Chuck. He apologised for the smell of smoke, as he had a woodstove running in the basement. As we entered the front door into the living room, the place definitely had wow appeal. The room was twenty-two feet wide and fifty feet long, with a sixteen-foot ceiling and a minstrel's gallery. It was impressive despite the fact that it was not finished. Wires were sticking out of the paneled walls, and numerous light fittings were sitting in boxes on the floor. The mantelpiece, which was a huge beam, was lying on the floor in front of the massive brick fireplace and wall that went up the full sixteen feet to the ceiling. Another huge beam lay in front of the brick fireplace in the kitchen. Yet another massive beam was holding up the ceiling in the fifty-foot-long kitchen. It was supported by three remarkably ugly steel teleposts. Outside was an enormous scrap heap with junk all over the place; it was going to take a lot of work to clean up the mess.

The house was built in 1979 but never finished properly. The owner built it as a retreat in the country, and apparently his wife hated it. They had split up, and he wanted to sell it. He gave us the full tour of the house and the substantial workshop. Jane and I thought it was wonderful, and the agent could not believe that we liked what she considered to be an awful place. Her problem was she had no imagination; both Jane and I could see the enormous potential, and finishing that place would be simple compared with the renovation we had done on the brick house.

By the time we had returned to the agent's office, Jane and I had decided that we wanted to buy it and asked her to arrange another appointment to see the owner so we could talk to him about it. She said that was not the way things were done. We should fill out the paperwork, making a formal offer, and leave a 10 percent deposit with the lawyer. I told her that it was imperative that I should see the owner because he would reject my offer out of hand, as I was not prepared to offer anything close to what he was asking. After threatening to go to a different agent if she was not prepared to make the appointment, she did what I asked and made an appointment to see him the next day.

We went in and sat at the kitchen table. Right away Chuck said, "I assume you want to steal this place for as little as possible?" I responded in the affirmative, adding that I in turn assumed that he wanted to "squeeze every last dollar he could out of me." He confirmed that my assumption was absolutely correct.

Right away we found that we were on the same page, and I asked what the property taxes were like. Immediately we were in a lengthy discussion about what a bunch of "blood-sucking leeches" all levels of government were and that there were taxes everywhere you turned.

As soon as we got back on the subject of his house being for sale, he turned to the agent and said, "Since I lowered the asking price, I am not prepared to reduce the price any further." The agent then said that she was not sure what the asking price was; could he please confirm it for us? I nearly fell off my chair when he said $190,000. He then turned to me and asked what I was prepared to pay, and I said $150,000. He said that was ridiculous and went on to explain that he had built the place with good-quality materials and you could not replace what he had built for less than $190,000, so that would make the 160 acres of land free.

Apparently, he had owned an auctioneering business and had been able to pick up all sorts of surplus building materials. He also had acquired a big load of one-inch plywood that he had used for the floors, which he then covered with one by fives and then hardwood.

The conversation went off in all directions with him telling me about all sorts of amazing things that he had come across as an auctioneer and also other business ventures he had been involved in. It was most interesting. I told him all about what we had been through with our nail business and how we were in the process of closing it down.

On returning to the subject of purchasing his house, I asked how long it had been for sale and how many people had been out to see the place. Apparently it had been up for sale for five years, and nobody had been out to see it, which was what finally convinced him to lower the price substantially. The estate agent added that she thought it was not only the high price but also the unfinished state of the house that had put everyone off. I told him what we had been through with the work we had done on the brick house so we should be able to handle finishing this one.

Obviously it was going to be an expensive proposition, so we could not afford to pay too much purchasing it. He would have to reduce his price a bit more. He came down to $170,000 and insisted that I should be willing to pay more, so I went up to $155,000.

Around this time Jane and Linda seemed to find something very amusing. In fact they had a complete laughing fit and had to leave the room. I did not even notice them go. I found out later that during my negotiation, I had kept saying, "Chuck, old boy," and they thought that was so funny. I kept telling him, "Chuck, old boy, if you don't make a deal with me today, you are never going to sell this place. I am the only person mad enough to take on the project, and you know it." Bit by bit he kept lowering his price all the while complaining that I was robbing him blind, and I kept raising my price little by little complaining that I really did not know how I was going to come up with the extra money.

About three hours had gone by, and we had reached the end of the road. Chuck had come down to $165,000 and reckoned I had stripped him "down to his underpants" and was going no further. I had raised my bid to $160,000 and could not go any further. We shook hands; I thanked him for his hospitality and said I would be in touch shortly.

On the way back to Linda's office, we discussed the situation and decided to fill out the paperwork, making an offer to purchase the property for $162,500, which we did right away. Chuck accepted our offer, and I phoned him asking if he would be good enough to allow us to pay him $102,500 right away and then have up to another year to pay the remaining $60,000 and interest on the outstanding balance. He agreed, and we bought the property and managed to have the total balance paid off in about four months.

In some respects, it felt like the whole Universal Nail adventure had been a bit of a failure, but in reality it set us up. It was only when we shut the business down that we realized the true enormity of capital we had tied up in stock. As we liquidated it all, we found that we were a lot wealthier than we had thought. The sale of the brick house paid the first $102,500, and the remaining $60,000 was easily paid for by sales of our nail inventory and the big nail machine, and that is another interesting story that I will now relate:

You will recall me mentioning that on the day that I purchased the machine for $5,000, the representative from Wafios had arrived at the Morrison factory a few hours after I had purchased and loaded the machine onto my truck. They phoned me immediately when I got home and offered me $10,000. They knew I had paid $5,000 and thought that doubling my money right away would be sufficient to get me to sell it to them. I refused, saying that I wanted to make nails with it and was not prepared to sell. A few months later, they phoned again and asked how much I wanted as they really wanted to purchase it. I let them know I would be prepared to sell it for $40,000. They said that was too much, but they were still prepared to pay $10,000. A few more months went by, and we had the same conversation yet again. By December 1984, I was no longer making any big nails so the machine was idle. I really needed cash to pay off the balance on the house purchase, so I called Wafios and asked if they still wanted to buy the machine. They asked how much I wanted for it. I told them $40,000, and they told me that was simply too much. What was my bottom line as they really were serious about buying it? Apparently they had a customer lined up who was impatient to take delivery. I said the lowest price I was prepared to accept was $30,000, and they agreed; that was $25,000 more than I had paid for it, and I had been able to make nails with it for a few years. It was a great deal, and the timing was perfect.

It was very handy to have that huge piece of equipment out of the way, as I was faced with the monumental task of getting rid of all of the machinery in preparation for selling or renting out the factory building.

With Granum being rather a quiet little town, it soon became apparent that I had no chance of selling the property for anything resembling a respectable price, so I went to plan B and set about finding someone to rent it. At that time the fertilizer plant in town was expanding and needed more space. As soon as I approached them and offered to rent the building to them, they were eager to move in.

The pressure was now on to clear everything out—quite a daunting prospect—but what was I going to do with everything? I had been contacting everyone I could think of who could help me sell the stuff. Over the years, I had dealt with a few industrial machinery dealers, and they were actively trying to find buyers for everything, but it was going to take time.

I decided that the best course of action was to strip all the machinery out of the factory, haul it up to our new property, and store it in our workshop until buyers could be found. At that stage, all my employees had gone and found alternative employment, so I was faced with doing it all on my own. I then thought of someone who might be able to help me.

In a nearby hamlet, there was an old, rather run-down garage and filling station operated by a very enterprising young man by the name of Albert McPherson. I explained the predicament I was in and asked if he would be prepared to work with me, dismantling everything and hauling it back to our new place. He agreed, and we set off for what was about to be a much greater adventure than we could possibly have imagined.

I drove down in the Universal Nail three-ton Dodge truck, and Albert took his one-ton breakdown truck pulling a two-axle, flat-deck trailer. The five-hour journey to the nail factory was fairly uneventful, and I parked the Dodge there and Albert parked his trailer. I then climbed into Albert's vehicle for the one-hour journey up to our cabin in the Porcupine Hills. The last mile of the journey, after leaving the municipal road, was along a very rough track and at an altitude of over four thousand feet above sea level. There was quite a lot of snow on the ground. We were driving up an incline, and there was a substantial snowdrift in the gateway ahead. Albert decided to charge it, as he thought he would be able to break his way through if he had enough momentum. We were going at a fair clip across incredibly bumpy terrain when we impacted the snow-drift. There was a tremendous "whoompff" and a total whiteout as the snow went right over the bonnet and windshield, and we found ourselves completely and utterly stuck. We had gone most of the way through the drift but had not quite made it through. Albert tried rocking the vehicle backward and forward in an attempt to get going, and there was a big bang and something vital broke. I seem to remember it was something to do with the spider gears.

That was it; there was nothing more we could do to get going until daylight. It was already quite late, dark, and about twelve degrees Fahrenheit. We were about a half mile from the cabin, so we loaded up with the essential items we needed and headed off. Making our way through the snow was very slow going. It was a beautiful night with enough moonlight to illuminate the spectacular scenery. There are no lights up there, and the only indication of human presence is a faint glow in the sky to the southeast from Lethbridge, which is about seventy miles away.

Cabin in the snow.

Arriving at the cabin was wonderful. In short order, we had the heating stove and the cookstove going. I cooked the dinner, and by the time we were eating it, the clock had reached one in the morning. We really enjoyed our dinner, and Albert still talks about that meal as being one of the finest he has ever eaten. The poor fellow was so tired that as soon as he finished eating, he sat in a comfortable chair by the stove and was asleep almost immediately.

The following morning, we had the full cabin-cooked breakfast and headed down to the truck. After considerable difficulty, we were able to dig it out, and Albert managed to get power to the wheels. He then drove the vehicle ever so gently the forty or so miles to the nail factory. A few calls on the factory telephone and Albert located the parts he needed in Lethbridge, and we drove off in the Universal Nail Dodge truck to pick them up. As soon as we got back to the factory, Albert was working on fixing his truck, and in next to no time it was back in action. We had a good look around the factory and made a plan of how we were going to dismantle everything and haul it back to our new place.

By then it was getting late, so we headed back up to the cabin. Having already cleared a trail to get back out of the snowdrift, we only had a small obstruction to clear in order to drive through. We parked the truck and shoveled for about twenty minutes, and we were able to drive through to the cabin. Dinner was served at a far more civilized hour that night, and we slept like the dead.

The next day, we were up bright and early and consumed the full cabin breakfast (egg, toast, bacon, sausage, tomato, hash brown pota-toes, and mushrooms). After that we were fully charged to work right through until dinner, and we really managed to get a lot done.

I started by disconnecting and unbolting the machines from the floor, while Albert took down the overhead hoists. By the end of the day, we had the Dodge loaded with nail machines and the tumbler, which was a full load. Albert's trailer had a stack of steel track and support structures for the overhead hoists, together with the two hoists, and strapped on top was the Datsun delivery truck. He was overloaded to say the least, but Albert did not seem too concerned.

We headed back to the cabin for dinner and a good sleep. The next day was about to be a memorable one for all the wrong reasons. After the full cabin breakfast, we went to the nail factory. Albert hitched on his overloaded trailer, I fired up the Dodge, and away we went. We had agreed that there was no point in us driving together, and we were going to drive straight through without stopping. Albert took off like a rocket and was out of sight within a few minutes. I went at a more sedate pace as the Dodge was at its most stable and economical if I travelled at about fifty to fifty-five miles per hour; also, I had a very valuable load on board and was determined to get it home undamaged.

As I was approaching Midnapore at the south end of Calgary, I spotted Albert's vehicle parked on the side of the road, so I pulled up behind him. Obviously the heavy load had been a bit more than one of his tyres could handle, as it had exploded and was completely shred-ded. As was normal for Albert, he was not carrying a spare tyre, so he set up a makeshift arrangement where he used a ratchet strap to pull that axle up from the ground so all the weight would be transferred to the other axle. It seemed to work, and off he went at great speed. Within a few minutes, he was far enough ahead of me that I lost sight of him in the traffic.

I drove through Calgary and was on the number two highway heading for Edmonton. I had just passed the turn for Carstairs go-ing up an incline, and as I reached the top, I could see Albert further ahead running toward me, waving and holding a bloody cloth over his mouth. I pulled up and stopped on the hard shoulder as Albert ran up to the truck. He was quite breathless and obviously highly stressed as he proceeded to tell me that he was overtaking a vehicle when a red Chevrolet pickup truck turned into his lane in an attempt to do a U-turn. He braked, but with an eight-ton load on board, it did not help much. He hit the truck, knocking it out of the way, and the trailer started jackknifing. That in turn caused him to lose control and leave the road into the grassy area between the divided highways. Travelling at about seventy miles per hour, he went down the dip and up the other side where his truck and trailer flew right across the two lanes going the other way. He impacted the crash barrier on the far side, demolishing about seventy feet of it before breaking through and careering down the embankment to a small creek bed.

According to an eyewitness who was driving the other way, Albert's vehicle flew across the highway several feet above the road as he approached. After taking out the crash barrier and thundering down the embankment, this witness stopped and looked down the slope. Shortly after coming to a halt, the truck door opened, and Albert came roaring out like a wild man all covered in blood. He ran up the hill shouting and swearing at the poor fellow, assuming that was the driver of the red truck. The police laid charges of "driving without due care and attention" and "attempting to make an illegal U-turn" on the driver of the red truck, but Albert paid the greatest price.

Albert was not wearing his seat belt but was holding the steering wheel so tightly that he had bent it into a U shape. During the impact, his face had hit the steering wheel and had cut right through the flesh beneath his nose, and his top lip was hanging off and bleeding profusely. He climbed into the Dodge, and I took the next exit off the highway to the hospital in Didsbury, where they sewed poor Albert back together.

Right after leaving the hospital, we went back to the crash site, climbed onto the trailer, which was still upright with everything in place, and removed the two hoists. We thought because they were valuable items and would be easy to run off with, we had better hide them. We dragged them off to a nearby clump of bushes and hid them in the undergrowth out of sight.

Dear Albert must have been in extreme discomfort but did not complain as I drove him home that day. During those few days, we truly bonded, and that was the start of an enduring friendship.

We managed to get all the machinery into the workshop where it sat for a few years. The first thing to sell was the Humphrey fence staple machine that I had purchased for $250 from the scrapman, which leads me to a story about an extraordinary man who was so honorable, I had never come across anyone quite like him before—or since, for that matter. His name was Bernie Smith, and he was from Connecticut. I'm not sure how I came across him, but I had known him for some time. We quite often talked on the telephone, but we never met. I had asked him to try to sell my equipment, and one day he phoned and said he had someone who wanted a fence staple machine; was mine in good work-

ing order? I told him it was. He asked how much I wanted for it, and I said $5,000. I asked if that was a realistic price, and he thought it was; he would see what he could do.

A few days went by, and he told me that his customer was going to buy it. He then gave me instructions on where

Jane with the Humphrey loaded to go.

to drop it off—to have it packaged and shipped at the customer's expense. The machine was duly shipped off, and a couple of weeks later a cheque arrived from Bernie; the cheque was written out for US$5,500. Right away I called Bernie to let him know that he had paid me $500 too much. He told me that he had asked the customer for $6,000, expecting to be beaten down on the price, and the customer had paid him the full $6,000 so he had decided to split the $1,000 with me.

What a truly remarkable man to have shared the windfall with me when most people would have just pocketed the full $1,000 and said nothing. When you consider that I had bought the machine for CAN$250, that was a wonderful price to get.

Sometime later all the remaining equipment was sold to a man by the name of Emil Tuescos, who was from Hungary. He was setting up a nail manufacturing plant there. He was delighted to be able to buy all the equipment he needed in one go and not have to pay very much. We sold him the entire package for $35,000, and I couldn't help thinking how wonderful it would have been if I had been able to purchase all that machinery for $35,000 in 1975.

He really did get an impressive deal, but there was no sense in me hanging on to the equipment any longer. As the fully loaded semitrailer pulled away that day, I felt a great sadness as that chapter of my life really was over.

Machinery leaving for Hungary.

(20)

FINAL THOUGHTS

WHEN I STARTED writing the story of the Granum Gripper, I was told by several people that I needed to end the story on a good note. That thought made me realize that although the day the machines fell silent would have been a logical place to end, it was far too depressing. That is why I continued a bit with "A New Beginning" to show how that decade of our lives had been a bit of a struggle but not without rewards, and we were ending it a lot wealthier than when we started—and not just in monetary terms. Far from being defeated, I was more confident than ever.

Shutting down Universal Nail was very hard to take, but I had come to realize that I was all right at making nails; however, that was not my real talent. My best attribute was that I could talk, and people liked me. The only reason the business was moderately successful was because of my ability to sell the product. I made a good product without doubt, but I certainly was not cheaper than everyone else; in fact I had quite a few customers who paid more for my nails not less. Looking back, it was the right decision as it freed me up to do far more interesting things that have resulted in meeting many incredible people and visiting numerous amazing places. I have been most fortunate.

I was working so much of the time that I felt sure I was missing opportunities where I could prosper more without working so many hours. On top of that, making nails had more than its share of dangers. I had experienced a few close calls, so maybe it was good to stop while I was still ahead. I had a nail fire out of a machine and stick in my cheek. I had a twelve-inch nail slice open my wrist. I turned the forklift over on its side, and the closest call of the lot was when a six-hundred-pound coil of wire crashed down onto the ground inches from my feet when the cable on the hoist snapped.

My perception of the world in 1985 had changed a lot from what it was in 1975. And yet I was only just beginning to get an understanding of how things really work. I had great difficulty understanding why innovation and hard work were punished, and laziness and failure were rewarded by governments. How could they be so stupid? Maybe they were not so stupid; I was assuming they wanted us all to prosper. How silly of me.

I have always been politically active, and during the last few years in Granum, I was a board member of the local constituency association of the federal Conservative Party. By observation it had been obvious to me that collectivism, whether it be outright communism or milder socialism, destroyed wealth wherever it had been the form of government.

What bothered me then and still does today is how people are so easily seduced by socialist principles and yet seem unable to understand that it is a guaranteed road to ruin. Collectivism, whether it be socialism or full-blown communism, not only has brought economic ruin to countless millions of people, but it has also been responsible for the mass murder of well over 100 million people who were slaughtered by their own governments. Far more people have died at the hands of their own governments than have died in all the wars put together. Very few people realize that. Search the word "democide" on the internet, and if the censors have not deleted it yet, you will find a study from the University of Hawaii, and it is a real shocker.

Remember, Communist Russia was "the Union of Soviet Socialist Republics." Nowhere in the name did the word "communist" appear. And by the way, the Communists did not go away when the Soviet Union "collapsed." Read Anatoliy Golitsyn's book *The Perestroika Deception* for details on that.

Because we are lied to about history (and a lot of other things too), we are told that the Russian working people rose up against the tsar and overthrew his government so the working people would be in charge and everybody would be free and prosperous. As we all know, that did not happen. The reality was that the banking elite in New York and London bankrolled and orchestrated the whole affair, and it had nothing to do with the Russian people at all. It was a foreign takeover in which a ruthless dictatorship was installed, resulting in the pillaging of the nation's wealth, the extermination of about 60 million or so innocent Russians, and the imprisonment of countless millions more. In order to have a clear understanding of what happened, Antony C. Sutton's book *Wall Street and the Bolshevik Revolution* is essential reading.

For significant wealth to be generated, you have to have individual liberty, and there must be a right to private property. Without those prerequisites, it is not going to happen. In a free society, people furthering their own self-interest will create the wealth, which lifts the standard of living for everyone. Of course a sound monetary system would be the icing on the cake, but don't hold your breath waiting for that to happen. A lot of brave men have ended up dead trying to do that. Another essential book to read to fully understand this phenomenon is Adam Smith's *The Wealth of Nations*. It is an old book but very valid.

A major problem faced by humanity is the ownership of the money system by a very small number of people. They create money out of nothing and lend it at interest. It is more than a little obvious that people with access to such unbelievable wealth could buy, and surely have bought, just about everything and everybody necessary to very nearly run the world. We know that their aim is one world government run by them, and with that thought in mind, so many random events happening in the world seem to have a common thread. They all help toward the centralization of power into fewer and fewer hands on the way to one dictatorial world government.

One essential element required is control of the "news," and what they call news is quite clearly information that *they* want you to know to further their agenda. If some event is not useful to their agenda, it will not be reported, or if they cannot get away with that, it will be grossly distorted and will not be anything like the truth.

So much of the so-called news is cherry picked or even staged to achieve some objective or other, which is why it is essential for everyone to understand "problem, reaction, solution," as it is employed all the time by the dark side of governments to get the general public to go along with things that they otherwise would not agree to.

The most obvious example of problem, reaction, solution is the tried and tested method used all over the world to remove the right of the general public to own firearms (victim disarmament). Out of the blue, some highly drugged nutcase (search "MK Ultra"), shoots some innocent victims, usually children. They can then blame the guns (not the drugs) for the tragedy and outlaw them. When you think about it for more than a few seconds, it is so obvious that something doesn't quite add up. Why would anyone hurt defenceless children? The answer is that nobody in his or her right mind would do such a thing; it is against human nature. That is why they have to be drugged and programmed to overcome their instinctive revulsion to harming children.

What would happen if there really were outraged people who were mad as hell for losing their jobs, homes, rights, or whatever? They would not shoot defenceless children; what is the point in that? They would take out authority figures, wouldn't they? People like politicians, judges, bankers, or executives of major corporations. Just think about how many potential crack-shot snipers there are who could easily drop

their victim from a quarter of a mile, and they only need one shot. We are talking about, at the very least, hundreds of thousands of potential assassins, and yet that does not happen because most people are essentially good. The few leaders who do get assassinated are always the good ones who are punished for helping their people and working against the globalist agenda.

I fully understand that what I am suggesting may sound outrageous, but please do me the favour of paying attention to the next mass shootings, and you will see the same pattern of events repeated again and again. Virtually every time, there are initially eye witness reports of multiple shooters, and then the story changes to the lone nutcase, who is a crack shot despite being drugged out of his mind.

As I said back at the beginning, on life's journey we are continually on a road with Y junctions, and every decision we make can have a profound effect on the future. I look back and, in some respects, it looks like a trail of wreckage as far as I can see, yet amongst all that wreckage, there have been some wonderful achievements and great experiences. The demise of the Granum Gripper was one of those sad moments, and yet experiences gained and friendships made during that time greatly enriched my life. I like to think that I have also had a positive effect on the people I have encountered along the way.

My father always used to say, "It is the people you help along the way that matters at the end of the day," and it doesn't necessarily have to be a big thing. That brings to mind a story that I should relate because it illustrates that point so well. It is a major diversion from nails, but I'm sure you will forgive me this transgression. In fact, if you have made it this far

Edward and Bruce Luckman

despite all the diversions, you will enjoy this one:

There I was in Zimbabwe (formerly Southern Rhodesia) in 1997 with my Australian gold prospector friend, Bruce Luckman. We were looking for a suitable location to set up an alluvial mining operation. We were having lunch with our geologist at the Miekles Hotel in Harare (Salisbury). As we were about to head off into the wilderness, I let them know that I was going to purchase some film for my camera while they were having their dessert.

I left the hotel and walked through a small park to reach a chemist shop (drugstore) on the other side. On my way, I noticed a young man sitting in a wheelchair beside a sheet of plywood covered in photographs. I went over to talk with him and asked what he was doing. As you see, in real life I go off on a few diversions here and there, and because of that, I have had more than my share of interesting experiences. You have to take time to smell the roses.

He told me that he had been in a car crash, and his back had been broken resulting in paralysis from the waist down. He was managing to eke out a living by taking photographs of passersby with his very decrepit camera, processing those pictures, and selling them to those people when they returned a few days later.

Because his camera was in such poor shape, only about half the pictures were satisfactory. The young man had a wonderful name that I'm sure I will never forget. He was called Togarepi Chimbaranga, and I thought about him a lot over the next few months.

Bruce had been back to Africa and claimed a stretch on the Mukuradzi River in the Mount Darwin area near the Mozambique border. (Having searched the rivers of Zimbabwe to make sure I have the spelling correct, I could not find it listed, so I might have the name wrong.) Bruce invited me to return with him a few months later to witness the initial test screening. I decided to go, and what a life-altering trip it turned out to be.

I had an old camera that I had bought secondhand in London back in 1972, and I no longer used it as I had bought a better one. I decided to take it with me and give it to Togarepi (if I could find him) along with some film.

At my first opportunity, I returned to the park where I had met Togarepi, and there he was.

He spotted me when I was about a hundred yards away and immediately started waving. I was so pleased to see him again, and I handed him the bag, saying I had a present for him that I felt sure he would like. He looked into the bag stuffed with film and did not notice the camera underneath, so I suggested he should dig deeper. When he pulled out the camera, he could hardly believe his eyes. It was a good-quality Chinon 35mm and always took first-rate pictures. He was so overwhelmed; tears were running down his face. We exchanged addresses so we could stay in contact.

A few weeks after my return to Canada, I heard from him, and he told me that all of the pictures were coming out perfectly and business had improved so much, people were hiring him for weddings and other events. Some months later, he wrote to say that business had been so good, he had been able to afford to lease a store where he had set up a studio. He was doing lots of weddings, and things were getting better all the time. A few more months went by, and he was doing so well that he was driving again and had a car that had been specially equipped with hand controls. He said that the business was thriving, and he was so grateful that I helped him get back on his feet. After a while, Zimbabwe descended into absolute chaos when the country's currency collapsed after hyperinflation rendered it worthless. I never heard from him again.

I mentioned that returning to Zimbabwe was the start of a life-altering trip. Well, seeing that I have headed off on this small diversion, let's keep on going now that I'm on a roll, and I'll tell you about what I was referring to.

On the long journey to Zimbabwe, I was reading *The Great Betrayal* by Ian Smith. He was a man whom I admired for his courage to defy Britain when standing up for his people. He was the last prime minister of Southern Rhodesia, and his book covered the events that led up to his government unilaterally declaring independence from Britain.

It went on to explain what happened after the declaration of independence. The mainstream media had told us how the people had risen up against his government and civil war had broken out, which resulted in negotiations with Britain. The book documented how those negotiations led to fraudulent elections and the consequent establishment of Communist black majority rule, which subsequently transformed a highly prosperous country into an economic basket case with little individual liberty.

Smith's version of what happened was very different from what the mainstream media had told us. The so-called civil war sounded more like an invasion of highly trained and armed foreign Communists. Although he did not directly claim that Britain was backing the Communists, it appeared that they were not concerned about the probability of allowing a Communist takeover of the country and at the time I read that, I found it very difficult to believe. Going to Zimbabwe, I thought that if I tried hard enough, I might just get a chance to meet him in person and talk with him about it.

The day it happened was one of the most memorable days of my life. My good friend Bill Frazier from South Carolina was with us, as he was one of the financial backers of Bruce's gold project. We were staying at the Dombawera Lodge, which was a wonderful place deep in the magnificent countryside. The evening before, we had climbed up a nearby kopje (rocky hill) to have a look at some rock paintings that had been there for thousands of years.

It was a beautiful morning, and a herd of elephants wandered past our cabins on their way to the watering hole as we were heading for the dining room. After a hearty cooked breakfast, we headed to Harare, and a mile or so down the trail to the road, a magnificent warthog ran out in front of our vehicle followed by a litter of piglets. They are so ugly that they are handsome. Beauty is indeed in the eye of the beholder. Truly magnificent creatures and it was a treat to have such a close encounter.

By noon we were back at the Bronte Hotel in Harare, and I suggested to Bill that we should find Ian Smith. By asking every white person I had come across since being in the country where I could find Ian Smith, I found out that besides his farm in the countryside, he also had a home in Harare where he spent quite a bit of time.

I hired a taxi driver and explained what I wanted to do. He was very good and agreed to give me a break on the cost as it was likely to be a time-consuming trip. We started by heading to an upscale residential area of the city, and we kept stopping to ask white people in the street if they knew where Ian Smith lived. As to be expected, despite everybody knowing the man, nobody seemed to have any idea where he lived.

Then we had a lucky break: this fellow told us that he lived on Phillips Avenue, but he did not know what number. We drove to Phillips Avenue, and of course, it went on for a long way. Again, we kept asking white people in the street, and they had no idea where on Phillips Avenue he lived.

Then we had another lucky break: We saw a fine-looking house with a wall around it and a security guard at the gate, and we asked him where Ian Smith lived. He knew right away and told us that his house was very near the Cuban Embassy, which was somewhere around 30 Phillips Avenue.

Our next stop was the Cuban Embassy where we asked again for directions and were directed to 33 Phillips Avenue. There it was: a very English-looking house with beautiful flowers in the garden. There were no walls or security guards. I walked down the garden path with Bill to the front door and knocked. My expectation was that if there were any answer at all, it would probably be a housekeeper. To my amazement, Ian Smith answered the door. I introduced myself and explained that I had been reading his book on the long journey from Western Canada, and I really wanted to talk with him about some of the things he had written about.

Right away he invited us in, explaining that he had only an hour to spare, as he had an appointment he had to keep later in the afternoon. We sat in his living room, and I had my chance to question him on the things that bothered me. I had always thought that Britain was opposed to Communism, so how could it possibly be that Britain made it so easy for the Communists to take over? What an eye-opener it was to listen to the man who was at the heart of that incredible piece of history. It was a major turning point in my life. If we had been told a pack of lies about that particular part of recent history, what were the chances that everything else was also a pack of lies? On leaving Ian Smith's home, we managed to get photographs with him, and I also got him to sign my copy of *The Great Betrayal*. Bill and I then headed to a great restaurant where we had crocodile for dinner. What an amazing day it had been.

On returning home, I embarked on a journey of discovery where I sought out books that would help me to connect the dots, so I could have a better understanding of real history rather than the version presented to us by the victors, and those with the money and power. That journey has not ended and never will; life is too short to have any chance of knowing it all.

We learn new things every day, and every person we meet has the potential to change our lives

Ian Smith and Edward.

for better or worse. There is a lot of evil in this world, but there is also a lot of good. Collectivism is such a terrible system, and the benefits of individualism are stupendous.

Ignorance is the greatest obstacle to a bright future, so we must all turn off the television and snap out of the trance we have been programmed into. Mainstream news is doing nothing more than brainwashing us into believing what those who are enslaving us want us to believe. We are lied to about almost everything; official history was written by the victors and is not the whole truth. We are divided and coerced into conflict amongst ourselves over things that just don't matter.

Wicked "false flag" atrocities like the events of September 11th 2001 are routinely staged to strip away vital liberties and justify unnecessary wars that kill millions of innocent people. This is no way to run the world. For anyone who still believes the official story, please check out the controlled demolition of building seven, proven beyond doubt by the experts at "Architects and Engineers for 9-11 truth." Also have a look at how the BBC reported the collapse over twenty minutes before it happened. Obviously they knew in advance that it was going to be demolished.

We really need to forget the forest and concentrate on the trees; it is individual people that count. Please take the time to check out Freedom Force International www.freedomforceinternational.org) and have a look at the Creed of Freedom. There is a huge awakening taking place. It is not enough to know what is happening; we have to make the commitment to snap everyone else out of his or her state of ignorance. There is no need for violence. A well-informed general public, capable of critical thought, who decide to resist the oppression is the greatest nightmare of the powers that be. Without our cooperation, they cannot totally enslave us; we are too many, and they are too few.

The hour may be late, but the fat lady has not yet sung. Let's take our liberty back.

Edward Goodliffe, July 2019

COMMENTS ON THE EXPERIENCE
OF WRITING THIS BOOK

THIS HAS BEEN a totally new experience for me, and there has been a whole lot more to it than writing the story. As you can imagine, documenting events that happened between thirty-four and forty-four years ago has its challenges. In fact some of the story goes back a full fifty years, and it is amazing what is stored away in our memories. There have been numerous things that I have not thought about for a very long time, and yet once I started concentrating on the book the memories came flooding back—names, dates, people, places. How could all that information be stored away for so long? It has been amazing to me, and the more I have thought about it, the more detail I have been able to recall, which has been incredibly handy when working on a project such as this. One of the great problems was getting the sequence right; did the Alberta Hotel burn down before or after we extended the factory building? Things like that have been difficult to pin down. In fact, I'm still not sure if Gary was in the factory with me on the day of the Alberta Hotel fire, and I have not been able to track him down to ask him. Inevitably, there must be things that I have forgotten, and I must have made mistakes, but I like to think that they are minimal and my representations of what happened are not too far off the mark.

Once I had essentially finished writing the story, I attempted to track down the people I had written about in the book—firstly to see if I had accurately portrayed the event that they were featured in, and secondly to see if they were happy to be included in the story. Again, it turned out to be quite a challenge. I have been reestablishing contact with people that I have not spoken with for a long time; in fact I can think of one whom I had not spoken to for forty years. The reaction of everyone has been very positive, and I have had some really great telephone conversations. Something that has been more than a little disturbing is the number of people who have cancer; have died of cancer; or have lost a spouse, brother, sister, in-laws, or children to the disease. Without doubt cancer is at epidemic proportions. Virtually everybody I have contacted has been affected in some way or another. This makes me realize the importance of us all knowing as much about this disease as possible, so we can firstly reduce our chances of getting it and, secondly, know what our options are for fighting it if we are unfortunate enough to be diagnosed with it. There has most definitely been suppression of treatments that have cured many thousands of people, and the information is available if you know where to look and have the motivation to do such a thing. A good starting point would be to go to www.cancertutor.com. If you want to know more about cures that have been suppressed, try searching Harry Hoxsey, Rene Caisse, Royal Raymond Rife, and Ernst Krebs Jr. That will lead you to others, and you will understand the enormity of the suppression. In my opinion the best book is *Cancer: Step Outside the Box* by Ty Bollinger.

Although closing down the nail factory was a great disappointment, I bear no ill will toward anyone, as all the apparent setbacks on life's journey always present new opportunities. Just imagine if Uncle George had not fired me from the family business all those years ago, how different my life would have been. That apparent setback might have been the greatest thing that ever happened. Good old Uncle George! Incidentally, I took the time to go back and visit him before he died to let him know that there were no hard feelings. In fact, I am most grateful for what he did; we just have to seize the opportunities when they arise, run with them, and see where they go. I feel sure that when we reach the end of the road, we will not regret the things we have done no matter how catastrophic they might have been, but we may well regret the things we did not do and should have.

Edward Goodliffe, August 2019

Jane and Edward.

CPSIA information can be obtained
at www.ICGtesting.com
Printed in the USA
LVHW051446160120
643761LV00003B/3

9 781977 215932